ENTERTAINING WITHOUT ALCOHOL

ENTERTAINING WITHOUT ALCOHOL

Dorothy Ruth Crouch

Arlington Books
King Street St. James's
London

ENTERTAINING WITHOUT ALCOHOL
First published in England 1986 by
Arlington Books (Publishers) Ltd
15–17 King St, St James's
London SW1

© *Dorothy Ruth Crouch 1985*
Originally published in the U.S.A.
by Acropolis Books Ltd, Washington DC 20009

Typeset in England by
Inforum Ltd, Portsmouth
Printed and bound in England by
Biddles Ltd, Guildford

British Library Cataloguing in Publication Data
Crouch, Dorothy
Entertaining without alcohol.
1. Carbonated beverages
I. Title
641.8'75   TP630

ISBN 0–85140–691–2

Acknowledgements

As with all big projects, this book is not the result of only my work. The dedicated efforts of many people made it possible.

Giuseppe Giustra, my contributing editor, worked many hours on the original manuscript. He did all of the preliminary editing, wrote the section about coffee, and made many additions to the manuscript. Giuseppe also patiently and repeatedly outlined the table of contents and kept track of sections that I needed to complete or expand.

In the early stages of manuscript preparation, Marie Smith Schwartz, who is the author of *Entertaining in the White House*, gave me excellent advice about how to research my topic.

Cheri Lofland, of the National Soft Drink Association, gave us numerous fresh ideas and was extremely helpful in providing us with recipes containing soft drinks.

Lois P., Helen T., Dottie C., and Sheila P. were an important resource group for me, providing contacts, helping me interview people, allowing themselves to be interviewed, and getting information for me about entertaining recovering alcoholics.

Jim Mallon, who kindly wrote the foreword to the book, then helped me further by following up on some statistical information that I needed.

Desmond Elliott not only provided me with the recipe of Bombe Desmond, but also for the outline for the final recipe for English Trifle. He also read the manuscript in its early stages and offered a number of helpful comments and suggestions.

I'd like to thank all of my friends and clients who made it easier for me to find the time to write this book by being willing to schedule appointments around the work, and for not getting angry because they hadn't heard from me for some time. Likewise, even though my family thought that I had gone off to another planet for the duration, they were very kind and supportive during the preparation of the book.

To all those people who talked to me about the book, and gave me anecdotes and ideas to be included in it, I say 'thank you, thank you.'

D.R. Crouch

Contents

FOREWORD
11

CHAPTER ONE
Why This Book?
15

How to Use This Book, 18
The Accidental Serving of Alcohol, 19

CHAPTER TWO
Some Special People
22

The Driver, Abstaining for the Event, 22
The Hostile Host/Hostess, 23
The Drinking Alcoholic, 24 .
Ideas from Recovering Alcoholics and Other
Nondrinkers, 26

CHAPTER THREE
Beverages
33

The Best of the Nondrinkers Favourites, 33
Mineral Waters, 33
Fruit Juices, 34
Alcohol-free Beer and Wine, 36
The Best of the Nondrinker's Favourites in Australia, 37
Alcohol-free Wine and Beer in Australia, 38
Teas and Coffees, 39

CHAPTER FOUR
Practical Substitutions and Alterations
43

Removing the Spirits Without Removing the Spirit, 43
What to use in place of light and dark rum, brandy, cordials,
red and white wine, sherry, etc., in sauces and desserts, 45
Poaching Liquids, 49
Braising Liquids for Meat and Poultry, 50

CHAPTER FIVE
Entertaining
52

The Cocktail Party, Large and Small, 52
The Tea in All its Glory, 56
Brunch: The New Cocktail Hour, 60
Breakfast: When Drinks are not Expected, 62
Lunch or Dinner, 62
After-Theatre Suppers, 67
The Saturday Night Party, 68
Basic Food Rules for Mixed Parties, 71
Business Entertaining, 76
Restaurant Dining, 92

CHAPTER SIX
Special Occasions – Ideas and Menus
96

New Year's Day, 97   Shrove Tuesday, 98
St. Paddy's Day, 99   Easter, 100
Whitsun Bank Holiday, 101   A Fancy Picnic, 101
August Bank Holiday, 102   Halloween, 103
Christmas Eve, 104   Christmas Day, 104
New Year's Eve, 105

CHAPTER SEVEN

Menus
108

Breakfast, 108
Brunch, 109
Lunch, 111
Dinner, 113.
Late-night Supper, 115
Spring Supper, 116

CHAPTER EIGHT

Recipes
117

Warm Greetings: Soups and Stocks, 117
Sumptuous Seafood, 125
Entrées: Dining Without Wining, 135
Assorted Specialities, 152
Savoury Sauces, Gravies, Marinades, 163
Tea for Two – or Twenty, 172
Here's to Good Friends – and zero-proof drinks, 179
The Vanilla Dilemma:
Substitutes for the Alcoholic Essence, 187
The Happy Ending, 190

APPENDIX
231

INDEX
234

Foreword

'The Way to Win is Not to Move'

I recently saw the film 'War Games' for the second time and was struck by the stark realism of the finale. Joshua, the computer, his alternatives exhausted by repeated attempts to win a nuclear war, accepts the inevitable— disengagement is the only viable alternative. This is also the healthiest attitude an alcoholic can have toward the use of alcohol.

The understandings of alcoholism are myriad, as are explanations of its cause. Sociologists differ from psychologists, physicians from clinicians and therapists. Yet each is studying the same phenomenon. The perspective determines the focus.

The professionals do agree, however, that alcoholism affects the individual's total life and negatively affects the family nucleus as well, and that alcoholism is a progressive malady. Continuing to drink, or returning to drink after a period of sobriety, guarantees deterioration. Unchecked alcoholism is fatal, at times directly so.

The professional's bias also influences his or her view of treatment, recovery, or control of alcoholism. Personally, I see alcoholism as a disease with clearly marked symptoms and stages, a definable etiology, and a reliable prognosis. Accepting this 'hypothesis'—in science there are no absolutes, only defensible theories—the alcoholic is a sick person whose long-term 'recovery' depends upon total abstinence from all mood-altering substances.

The immediate treatment process differs according to the progression of the disease in the individual. The range of possibilities extends from 'cold turkey-ing-it' to hospitalization for detoxification with follow-up residence in a rehabilitation treatment facility ranging from 21 days to 6 months or more.

The advantages of the view of alcoholism as a disease include the psychological boost to the client, who begins to see himself/herself as a sick person trying to get well, rather than bad person trying to be good. This also ends the useless tension of trying to control the intake. In any event, attempting control is an exercise in futility for the alcoholic. As Alexander Pope wrote, 'To know ourselves diseased is half our cure.' When recovering alcoholics narrate their experiences with alcohol, they talk about 'crossing the invisible line' into uncontrollable drinking. In medical terms this parallels the concept of the tolerance level. Determining an individual's tolerance level for alcohol is next to impossible. The tolerance for alcohol at first increases and then unpredictably drops off; at that point the individual has become physically addicted to and mentally obsessed with alcohol. Loss of control has nothing to do with quantity. It means that the alcoholic cannot regularly predict what will occur when he/she drinks. 'Loss of control' is the characteristic symptom of alcoholism.

Although several research efforts suggest the possibility of re-education to social drinking for the alcoholic, there is as yet no solid evidence of success.

There is simply no cure for alcoholism at this writing. The hope for the alcoholic is that the disease can be permanently arrested and its doleful consequences checked. This hope is rooted in total abstinence— avoidance of all alcohol intake. To begin the measuring game is to play Russian roulette, and the alcoholic always loses the struggle with alcohol, which is a cunning and patient adversary.

Total abstinence means avoiding alcohol altogether. In our society that is not an easy task. Social life centres around alcohol to an alarming degree. Alcohol—in varying percentages—is also an integral part of items in daily use; e.g., mouthwash. The nonalcoholic beverages, which are not the same as 'no-alcohol' beverages, pose a more subtle threat. They do include some fermented fruit and at times include up to .05 percent alcohol. Perhaps this is not enough to be noticed, or legislated. The alcoholic's system is not versed in chemistry or law, however, and for some individuals less than a little is too much. For example: cooking with alcohol may in fact burn off the alcohol content of a dish, but the taste lingers on. This can be hazardous.

As Joshua, the computer, spelled it out, 'the only winning move is not to play.'

In light of this message, the book *Entertaining Without Alcohol* is a real contribution. It takes the 'disease' concept quite seriously and yet is permeated with real sensitivity for the recovering alcoholic.

Dorothy Crouch has shown that half-measures are not necessary and that recovering alcoholics need not become recluses. When the host or hostess becomes sensitive to the needs of these guests, a gradual change becomes evident in social gatherings. This book is a giant step in that direction.

Entertaining Without Alcohol is a much-needed book. It reminds us of the importance of being actively aware of the total sensibilities of our guests. It also reminds the recovering alcoholic that there is no need to stock alcohol in one's home in order to entertain successfully. *Entertaining Without Alcohol* is a milestone and deserves the highest recommendation.

James P. Mallon, S.T.D., C.A.C.
Director, Residential Programs
Addictive Diseases Center
James C. Giuffré Medical Center
Philadelphia, Pennsylvania.

CHAPTER ONE

Why This Book?

This book is written to help you entertain successfully without serving alcohol. You may be, as I am, the average host/hostess discovering that more and more of your guests are not drinking. This is happening for a variety of reasons. They may be recovering alcoholics (who may themselves wish to begin entertaining again), physical fitness enthusiasts, expectant mothers concerned about both their health and that of their babies, and others who abstain for religious or health reasons.

This is what happened to me. First, I had a good friend who embarked on the journey toward recovery from alcoholism; then a few more cut down or cut out their drinking following intensive exposure to the mirror of physical fitness; then I met another recovering alcoholic who in turn introduced me to others who no longer drink. As my association with these delightfully interesting people grew over a six-month period, I changed my entertaining style from basically planning for drinking occasions to arranging basically nondrinking ones. Then an old, dear friend had to give up alcohol, salt, and sugar—virtually everything, or so I mourned—due to serious health problems. As cheer therapy against bitterness I gave a formal dinner party for him and invited all the people I thought would be able to enjoy a nondrinking evening. I got a big surprise! It was more fun than the familiar barrel of drunks.

At first I tried with diabolical cunning to duplicate

alcoholic beverages without the booze, not realizing that I was only making it more difficult for my recovering alcoholics to tell the difference. As for cooking with alcohol, it never occurred to me that not only should I prepare dishes without alcohol, but that I should also abandon all hope of ever being able to cook out the devilish stuff, for the residual taste of booze does not leave, and why should it? That's what it's there for in the first place.

I had to find a way. There must be a way, I fumed. I became obsessed. I went to those who can't drink. Since they are the most sensitive to, and must observe strict rules for avoiding the least drop of, alcohol, they became my control group for my endless experiments with nonalcoholic entertaining. If they could enjoy what I was doing, other nondrinkers would, too, I decided. And much to their astonishment, so did many of my drinking friends.

My nagging questions during some of these conversations concerned how to entertain without alcohol and whether it was possible to redesign dishes that my friends could no longer eat. I started experimenting with traditional recipe favourites to see if I could capture the excitement of the original recipe without retaining the stubborn booze taste. Yes, indeed, it can be done! The vanilla controversy was brought up (see *The Vanilla Dilemma*); I went to work on alternatives. My friends have cheerfully acted as guinea pigs, tasting the dishes and letting me know what worked and what didn't.

At about this time, I went looking for a cookery book to help me convert recipes. I could find nothing whatsoever on the subject, and certainly nothing about how to entertain mixed groups of drinkers and non-drinkers. The assumption seems to be that nondrinkers can fend for themselves within the larger group of drinkers. This of course is true; nondrinkers manage to avoid alcohol even when surrounded by it. But the times, as always, are a-changing. It is no longer *chic* to be a heavy drinker; today's lifestyle is one of action, and as we all know, you can't be totally active when you're slightly hung over. I'm convinced this is true for daily drinkers (including myself) who don't notice the debilitating effect of the sauce until they cut back and realize how much more energy they have, how much sharper their minds are. Also changing is the law, which is imposing stiffer penalties in an effort to fight the problem of drunk drivers. It is also true that hosts and hostesses are giving more attention to guests who must drive home, being only too aware of the difficulties involved in the loss of a driving licence, which invariably occurs if one is caught driving after a few drinks (and it only takes very few). They are also showing a greater concern for the preferences of their nondrinking guests, whether this status is permanent or temporary.

This book was inspired by a special category of reader: the recovering alcoholic who is ready to begin entertaining again but doesn't know where to start. So many people told me that once they stopped drinking they stopped entertaining. In many cases they avoided French restaurants like the plague—the plague that alcoholic sauces had become to them. Once upon a time their social events had been centred around drinking. Now, they wondered, was there entertaining after sobriety? They were often at a total loss. One woman confided that her recipes had alcohol in them so that she could keep on drinking while she cooked. She's sober now, and still cooking; but only the food is sauced! She's using almost every one of our ideas for 'how to' without alcohol.

Whether you or your guests are on the wagon permanently or for the occasion, we believe you'll find useful suggestions in these pages for entertaining—successfully and enjoyably—without alcohol. One small warning: you may discover that without alcohol your 'appetit' is more 'bon' than ever!

How To Use This Book

The recipes that follow are largely limited to those that normally tend to include wine or other alcoholic ingredients. I'm sure you already have several of the many good cookery books that cover the basics and feature the standard recipe categories. So the focus here is on converting alcohol-containing recipes into successful nonalcoholic versions—removing the recipe's 'spirits' without removing its spirit! We hope you will be inspired to alter them as you probe and taste, and to let us know of your triumphs for the next edition.

A recipe is given for each of the starred dishes in the menu listings. We hope you also find that these dishes have star *quality*. Many of the recipes are for a particular class of dish. You can use them as guides in creating your own versions for 'the cause.'

Anecdotes from other pioneers who have muddled through the process of learning to entertain groups comprised of both drinkers and nondrinkers are highlighted in chapter two, which also relates the experiences of those presiding at their first totally alcohol-less affairs. This section is one of my favourites because it's so fascinating to hear about these individual experiences, which illustrate the different points of view and approaches to nonalcoholic entertaining.

We have tried to present recipes whose ingredients are easily obtainable at your local market. Where exceptions were necessary, such as in the case of nonalcoholic wines, we've listed sources in the Appendix. Happily, we found the distributors of these products more than cooperative in providing this information.

We have also tried to avoid having you rush out to buy costly, fancy kitchen appliances in order to polish your skills in the area of booze-free cuisine. Food processors can be a great help, but puréeing can also be accomplished in a blender or food mill without undue drudgery. We're assuming you have the basic kitchen equipment, and have listed the equipment needed for each basic recipe. If you're careful to read the whole recipe before you start, producing the desired result should be a breeze.

Menus are in a separate section to make them easy to find. All of the recipes are organized by category, and alphabetized in the index. General comments on a particular food or type of cooking appear at the beginning of the appropriate section, and we've made the table of contents very specific for ease in finding topics and dishes of special interest.

The Accidental Serving of Alcohol

The jokes that crop up here and there in this otherwise earnest book may be unnerving to some, but past, present, and recovering alcoholics tend to treat the topic that way, we've found. If you were to drop in on your local AA meeting, you'd hear gales of laughter emanating from the clouds of smoke and aroma of coffee. There are gripping silences, too; the very special silences when the room reverberates with the sharing of a moment recounted and painfully relived by those assembled. These poignant moments have the depth of prayer. But then comes the laughter, the inevitable laughter, the buoyant sound of those who are shaping better futures by sharing difficult pasts.

Is it true that deadly serious alcoholics—those who find it hard to laugh at themselves or at life's assorted tragedies—too quickly find themselves seriously dead?

But let's get at least mildly serious here. What about the accidental alcoholic encounter—when some well-meaning soul inadvertently provides a potentially disastrous stray serving of alcohol to one who cannot tolerate it? What to do? What does—or should—happen when a recovering alcoholic or nondrinking person is accidentally served a drink and downs it before recognizing its lethal properties?

The question is certainly less compelling than whether humanity can survive a nuclear holocaust. The prospect of such an occurrence can, however, raise an alcoholic's panic level to impressive heights.

The unasked-for alcohol is unexpectedly on the tongue. The action of our scenario is then determined by its star:

- If our victim is an active drinker, he or she smiles.
- If our victim is already drunk, he or she grins—a fool's grin: there is no other expression quite like it in the world.
- If our victim is a nondrinker, he or she becomes monumentally annoyed.
- If our victim is a recovering alcoholic, he or she has a real problem:
    — to swalloweth or not to swalloweth;
       to spitteth out or not to spitteth out;
       and what price pride?

As our stars play out their roles, the controversy over their options rages on. Some observers contend that the accidental ingestion of a dose of the demon brew will send you neither to heaven nor to hell. As long as it was *unintended*. But if the alcoholic has recently been detoxified or is relatively new to sobriety (and/or is still in the middle of a soulful internal battle over whether or not he/she is or isn't), it can be quite serious.

Fortunately the host/hostess is not on trial. You cannot be omnipresent, sniffing every drink, testing every plate, rolling back the eyelids of your guests to examine the shine of their eyeballs. In any event, ex-boozers always sniff strange stuff first and cautiously taste the initial bite. It becomes second nature. Animals do it as a matter of course, for they are responsible for their fate. So, in the final analysis, are recoving alcoholics. You are not.

However, you *are* responsible for doing everything possible, taking every possible step, making every possible arrangement to insure that your recovering alcoholic's fate remains in his or her hands and not in the chance clutches of an accidental serving of alcohol.

Even so, you may find some of my precautions a bit drastic. You may even find them amusing, but remember, they're less than hilarious to the recovering alcoholic. I hope these individuals recognize them as expressions of my love for them, which I ask you now to share with me.

CHAPTER TWO

Some Special People

The Driver—Abstaining for the Event

Scandinavian countries are notable for a long tradition of expecting the driver to stay sober on festive occasions. We are only now beginning to share this tradition in the grim aftermath of numerous road tragedies. Increasingly strict drunk-driving laws are also playing a role. As people realize how little alcohol it takes to jeopardize driving safety, many now avoid drinking altogether before driving.

Most of these individuals are 'social' drinkers who stay dry because they are driving. Because these people can enjoy 'nonalcoholic' beer and wine (which actually contain a small amount—.05 percent or less—of alcohol), you do not need to be concerned about wine or spirits in food served to them; they enjoy freedom of choice in this regard. They can take it *and* leave it, unlike alcoholics, who must either take it or leave it.

As a host/hostess, the best thing you can do for your drivers is to make it as easy as possible for them to avoid alcohol and still join in the fun of the event. This means that at a sit-down lunch or dinner you will offer a nonalcoholic beverage to the entire group so that your driver doesn't have to search out the alcohol-free beverage or make do with water. Of course, if you have recovering alcoholics among your guests, you will be serving a number of truly (100 percent) alcohol-free beverages as well as alcohol-free food. At a big party you'll definitely have recovering alcoholics in attendance, making it essential to have a dry bar* for anyone who doesn't want to drink, regardless of the reason.

These nondrinking drivers, having agreed to avoid alcohol and perhaps finding it more difficult to stay sober in a festive setting than they had expected, appreciate your care. So do a lot of might-have-been widows and orphans.

The Hostile Host/Hostess

For some reason, known best to the guilty parties, some people just can't seem to accommodate their guests' allergies with any real graciousness. These people are unquestionably dangerous to recovering alcoholics in that they will swear that there is no alcohol in a given food or beverage when there in fact is, on the incorrect assumption that a little bit won't hurt. If you are a recovering alcoholic, give your host a second chance after you've explained that 'a little bit does indeed hurt.' If this doesn't work, don't eat at that person's house again.

At a sit-down event, you are very much at the mercy of the host even if you bring your own bottle of mineral water. You must still eat the food as prepared or go hungry, and life is too short to spend it pushing alcohol-laden food around your plate. If you're willing to risk this well-meaning person's house at all, we suggest attending big parties where there will be a variety of food and drink. Bringing your own bottle of nonalcoholic beverage along is fair even though the event may be an elegant

---

* In this book the term 'dry bar' means the bar which serves only completely alcohol-free drinks. All others are served from the 'wet bar', even those containing minute quantities of alcohol.

one. This resistant kind of person has been known to pre-mix the rum and cola and put it back into the cola bottle.

Some of the people I have labelled hostile aren't so much hostile as ignorant of the effect a little alcohol can have on a recovering alcoholic. A good analogy is that of the danger of shellfish to a person who is violently allergic to it. The only difference is that the person who eats the offending shellfish may have to be taken to the hospital within twenty minutes of doing so, while the recovering alcoholic may not react until it is too late for such conveniences as hospitals. The two allergies are equally deadly.

If you would like to learn more about the physical aspects of alcoholism we suggest you contact the publishing division of Alcoholics Anonymous who have a large number of publications on the subject and will know what to recommend. The address is Alcoholics Anonymous, 11 Redcliffe Gardens, London S.W.10.

The Drinking Alcoholic

Every host/hostess has had at least one or two experiences with the actively drinking alcoholic. For any number of reasons, you may not want to eliminate these persons from your guest list, but they clearly present a problem and you dread their arrival at your parties.

From my point of view, the biggest problem is the distinct and unpleasant personality change that often takes place as the level of intoxication rises. Some of these drinkers seem to cross an invisible line, at which point you must deal with a monster in your house. My initial reaction always used to be one of fear until a friend who is a recovering alcoholic made the following suggestion: 'Find something to compliment the person about. This something *must be true*, as drunks are super-sensitive about what they believe is and isn't true about themselves. Keep complimenting the person until their anger is relieved.'

The rest of his advice centred on the reasons for the anger itself. A person who is drinking out of control may realize that this is happening and become increasingly angry and embarrassed at losing control of mental and physical functions. This anger can eventually be directed outward at others at the gathering. By flattering the enraged drinker's attributes, or actions (say anything complimentary as long as it's true), you may defuse the anger.

If your walking (staggering?) time-bomb guest wants a drink, give it to him/her. This is no time to discuss the person's drinking. You may be able to divert this deter-mined drinker slightly with sweets, but don't count on it. An alcoholic will not be diverted for long.

If this person is a guest at a sit-down dinner, you may place a *long-term* recovering alcoholic either next to or across from him so that they can converse. Recovering alcoholics of long standing are very gentle and sym-pathetic with drinking alcoholics in a social situation. However, you should consider possible personality con-flicts, as you do in any case. There are many sorts of drunk.

Be prepared to make arrangements to get the drinker home after the event. Do this tactfully so that it appears that persons A and B just happen to have room in their car and are happening to drive in the right direction. Let someone else drive the drunk's car home if he/she has one. Whatever you do, do not let this person get behind the wheel and drive. As a last resort, disable his/her car so it won't start. One way to accomplish this is by discon-necting the distributor cap; another is by putting a potato up the exhaust pipe! (The car will start but will quickly die out). Consult your local mechanic on other ways to love the drunk and his potential victims.

Ideas from Recovering Alcoholics and Other Nondrinkers

'Half of them are nondrinkers. Help!'

'None of my friends are drinking anymore. What do I do?' If I heard this comment once, I bet I heard it 50 times in the course of talking to people about this book and the new kind of entertaining it represents. Hitherto most of my friends seemed to fit in one of two categories—those who didn't drink at all because they were 'never-drinkers' and those whose social gatherings routinely included alcoholic drinks. The never-drinkers had a whole repertoire of menus, party styles, and friends who also abstained. When I visited these friends, it was under-stood that there would be no alcohol served—none in the beverages and none in the food. Several of these people chose to avoid serving caffeine, so the drinks were usually fruit punches of various varieties, or hot and cold herbal teas.

One thing that stands out in my memories of parties thrown by never-drinkers is that there was a lot of food and that it was very good food. By contrast, my friends who were fairly heavy drinkers accented the alcohol—they automatically offered you a drink the moment you crossed the threshold and were unhappy if you didn't take one. The food at their parties was good, but secondary to the drinks, which were strong and plentiful. By the time the late night buffet would appear, I would sometimes be too tired to eat.

Over the course of my work on this book, I've had the opportunity to talk to many friends and friends of friends about just how they entertain. One couple, who live in California, are just now, in the last six months or so, making a determined effort to change their drinking habits. They found that by the time they finished pre-dinner cocktails, wine with dinner, and post-dinner liqueurs, 'we were too blitzed to do anything but continue drinking for the rest of the evening.' These two are athletic and fit, arising at 5 a.m. to run, after which they return to put their house in order before shooting off to high-powered jobs, so they hardly fit the stereotype of heavy social drinkers. Their solution to the problem of changing their habits is to have dinner earlier, then plan some evening entertainment that will appeal to their guests. This varies from board games to charades, or might be an evening of serious discussion such as the one thoughtfully planned for me on my last visit. Pre-dinner drinks are no longer necessarily alcoholic and no pressure is put on guests to drink. To the best of my knowledge, there are no recovering alcoholics in this particular group, so no attempt is made to keep alcohol out of the food, but mineral water is available along with the wine at dinner. Just having it there makes it easier to cut down on the amount of wine consumed.

Changing entertaining styles

Another friend, who is a recovering alcoholic, said that when she stopped drinking she had to change her way of entertaining completely. First, she had to select nearly all new recipes since the old ones were loaded with alcohol. She now prefers not to have booze in the house, although she will serve drinking guests a drink if they want it. She also suggests that drinkers bring their own bottle and depart with the remains. Ditto if they want wine with dinner; they are welcome to bring it and then take the leftovers home. It is important to her not to be 'apart from' but 'part of' and she sees no reason for the fact that she doesn't drink to set her apart. Therefore, unlike many of the recovering alcoholics I talked to, she entertains frequently. She is also recognized by all as an excellent cook. She likes the elegance of stemmed wine glasses, but as she says, 'I discovered you can drink other things out of wine glasses.'

Shortly after she became sober, she threw one of her first parties and made another discovery: her drinking friends didn't expect to drink at her house anymore. She says 'I had gone to some considerable trouble to obtain individual-size bottles of wine and booze for my drinking guests so that they could drink even though I didn't. They explained that they would be just as happy without the alcohol, that they had come to enjoy the company.' Since then, she has switched to bring-and-take-your-own bottle, which works fine. In a restaurant, she will eat a sauce if the alcohol has been completely cooked out, but no longer cares for the taste of alcohol-based dishes. She had one last comment to make, and of all of the people I talked to, was the only one to focus directly on just this point. She says, 'If there is anything I would like people to know about recovering alcoholics, it is that we aren't weird and that, contrary to popular belief, we're not against alcohol, except for ourselves.'

Suggestions from never-drinkers

Here are some thoughts that were shared with us by the General Conference of Seventh-Day Adventists, who are never-drinkers. One particularly interesting type of dinner they suggest is the 'taco buffet,' with all of the different taco toppings and condiments served in separate bowls for guests to use in building their individual creations. Another fun idea is the dessert get-together that features a fondue pot of bubbling hot chocolate sauce for guests to dip chunks of fruit and cut-up pieces of sponge cake into. To a chocoholic such as I this sounds like heaven. My favourite fruit for dipping is tinned mandarin orange segments, followed quickly by slightly stale sponge cake. Not incidentally, there's a great chocolate sauce in the dessert section, which just happens to be thick enough for chocolate fondue.

Two other nondrinking friends say they always have

coffee on tap at all times during their parties. They, too, had to revamp their recipe files after they stopped drinking to eliminate the ones with alcohol. This couple kindly gave me their discarded booze-ridden recipes so that I could experiment with efficient and tasty booze-removal. One of the successful results, the chicken/duck liver spread, is also here for you to try. They both stay strictly away from wine-based sauces as they have found that the taste can trigger the urge to drink even when all the alcohol has been cooked out. When they talked to me about the recipes I was preparing for this book, they said 'don't try to duplicate the booze-filled recipe exactly; we don't want to find ourselves eating any recognizable booze-flavoured sauces.' When they occasionally throw fairly large business parties, they set up the wet bar with bottles borrowed from a friend, returning the leftovers immediately after the party. Their party menu is alcohol-free, so guests don't need to worry about alcohol in the food. Since they do a fair amount of entertaining, they are often in touch with other partygivers, which has given rise to a pet peeve: the host who says 'this is my favourite recipe and I don't know any other way to do it.' This comment inevitably means that there is booze in the dish, and that maybe they can't have it, depending on whether or not the booze has been eliminated in the cooking process. Given their views on wine-flavoured sauces, they might not want to eat it even then. They also advise anyone who is concerned about alcohol content to become a very careful label-reader.

Recent Mummy changes more than nappies

A friend of mine who is a recent mother gave up her usual glass of wine with dinner and drink or two at parties during pregnancy and while she was breast-feeding. During that time, she found it convenient to make quick stir-fry dishes in a wok that had been given to her as a wedding gift. Some of the dishes were Chinese, others were her versions of various vegetable dishes. I recently asked her about how she was entertaining these days and whether or not she had returned to her former style of serving wine with dinner. She told me that, much to her surprise, she hadn't returned to her original style, but that a new, much lighter style had evolved from her experience. An additional surprise was that she had lost her taste for alcoholic beverages. She now serves many more vegetable dishes, more chicken and fish, and most often, a herbal tea, either hot or cold, with the meal. Guests came to expect a nonalcoholic service when she was pregnant, and she says that there is no pressure on her now to return to her former patterns.

Hosting recovering-alcoholic style

I recently attended a very festive birthday party which was hosted by a group of recovering alcoholics for drinking and nondrinking friends. Immediately noticeable was the large pot of coffee brewing in the centre of the serving counter. The hosts made and served hot tea as well. The only alcoholic drink served was white wine, which was kept out of sight in the refrigerator. Those who wished to enjoy it helped themselves to clear plastic glasses and then helped themselves to the wine. This allowed the host to avoid the necessity of handling the open wine bottles in order to provide for his drinking guests. The matter of handling open bottles of alcoholic drinks came up repeatedly in my talks with recovering alcoholics. I have yet to meet one who was comfortable handling an open bottle, and many are not even comfortable with the sealed bottles. Various kinds of cold soft drinks were served, all in waxed paper cups. As I have come to expect at parties given by recovering alcoholics, there was a lot of food; it was out when the guests arrived, and more food kept coming out of the kitchen.

This party was a buffet, with a menu that ran from hors d'oeuvres to birthday cake. All you needed to do to enjoy all the courses was to stay at the party. In reasonably prompt succession, each course marched out of the kitchen, was devoured, and replaced by the next course. Great party, good company, and no particular pressure to drink.

Airline travel: flying too high

Now that it's chic for airlines to try to make everything upmarket and 'gourmet,' I noticed on a recent flight that both of the entrée selections offered in tourist class contained wine or spirits. The first option was beef braised in wine and the second, chicken in a pear sauce that included pear liqueur. While I am sure that in both cases the actual alcohol was cooked out, the beef still tasted strongly of burgundy and the chicken had a definite liqueur overtone. On another flight, earlier in the day, the choice had been better. One could choose between an omelette made with no alcohol, a quiche Lorraine, also acceptable, and a seafood Newberg made with a brandy cream sauce. At least on this flight, it was possible to avoid the alcoholic food. More and more, travellers are learning to discuss the menu with the airline when reservations are made. Most airlines are happy to provide special meals if they are requested to do so in advance. But don't expect their representatives to understand the subtleties of the difference between an alcohol-free sauce and a sauce that has all the wine cooked out of it but is still not wanted by a recovering alcoholic. It's a very strange idea to most people, who have had no reason to think about it, and it takes some patience on your part to get it across.

'Monitoring' recipes for alcohol content

A recent perusal of what used to be called the 'women's

pages' and are now called lifestyle or living pages of several newspapers revealed a high proportion of recipes that contained wine and/or spirits. A welcome change from this tendency are the recipes in the Christian Science Monitor, which are very good and, except for the use of vanilla and other extracts, can be counted on to avoid the use of alcohol. The same is true of the excellent recipes in *Here's Health Magazine*. I know that other health-oriented periodicals also make a point of excluding alcohol from their recipes. These are good sources of new dishes and are highly recommended.

CHAPTER THREE

Beverages

The Best of the Nondrinker's Favourites

The reaction of some of the friends we talked to about this book to the thought of entertaining without alcohol was 'what else is there to serve'?' The purpose of this chapter is to answer just that question.

The acceptable beverages will be separated into two categories: dry and slightly wet. The only beverages you may safely serve to recovering alcoholics are those in the first category, which do not even contain a tiny amount of alcohol. We have excluded carbonated soft drinks such as Colas and Lemonades as there is a wide choice, all easily obtainable. The suggestions in this chapter are all for drinks which we feel will complement our rather formal meals when the usual coffee, tea or soft drink won't do.

Firstly sparkling or 'fizzy' mineral waters. These have now become very popular here and there are any number of brands available in your supermarket or wine shop, both imported and home grown (if that is the word for water). Most people will drink whatever mineral water is offered with a meal, with or without the slice of lemon or lime. Fizzy mineral water mixes well with fruit juice to produce a light refreshing drink with less sweetness and fewer calories than the pure juice. A spritzer made with fresh apple juice and mineral water is excellent at any time of day.

There are many brands and flavours of pure fruit juices available, both still and sparkling. Here are some suggestions, all of which are suitable to serve at parties:

The Copella Farm Range –   Pressed Apple
Pressed Apple with Strawberry
Pressed Apple with Guava
Morello Cherry with Apple
Pressed Blackcurrant with Apple
Pressed Blackcurrant with Apple

These are nicely bottled but are perhaps not very suitable to serve with the food as they are on the heavy side. These juices are excellent as an aperitif, however, and can be found in supermarkets and health food shops.

Schloer –   Sparkling Apple Juice
Sparkling Red Grape Juice
Sparkling White Grape Juice

Schloer was, we believe, the first company to introduce an acceptable alcohol-free alternative to champagne to this country in the form of its sparkling apple juice. *Schloer* now also do the sparkling red and white grape juices and all three products are excellent. Available in supermarkets and larger branches of *Boots*.

Francere –   Sparkling Apple Juice
Sparkling Red Grape Juice
Sparkling White Grape Juice

These are very appealingly bottled and would not look (or taste!) out of place at a formal dining-room table. Widely available.

Schloss Heidelberg –   Red Grape Juice (still)
White Grape Juice (still)
Apple Juice (still but clear)

These are also very attractively bottled and are a good substitute for still wine. Available in *Holland and Barrett* and other health shops.

Two other types of sparkling apple juice, which also have the advantage of being packaged in individual-sized bottles, are *Appletise* and *Kiri*. These are often to be found in even the smaller soft drink outlets.

There are too many different brands of still fruit juices in cartons to mention them all here but it is definitely worth noting the *Lindavia* range. There are eighteen different flavours in the range, many of which are exclusive to *Lindavia*. These juices are unfortunately not yet very easy to find in this country. Check the Appendix for the address of the distributors, *Leisure Drinks* and contact them directly if you have trouble finding the product.

Lastly in the dry category, we must mention *Original Old Norfolk Punch*. This is made to a mediaeval monastic recipe and contains herbs of great potency and strength (without alcohol) steeped in the natural underground waters of Welle Manor Hall in Norfolk.

The makers today make no medicinal or curative claims but they do say:

'Throughout the Middles Ages everyone relied upon the curative properties of herbs for the relief of their ills, including 'lowness of spirits'. It was a natural progression to add alcohol and so give rise to our modern version of punch. Old Original Norfolk Punch contains no alcohol yet warms and uplifts the spirits in a vastly superior way.'

Equally good served ice-cold or piping hot, this truly non-alcoholic beverage is available in many branches of *Holland and Barrett* or through the producers (see Appendix).

Now to the second category. Slightly wet beverages. We, in Great Britain, are not nearly as well prepared to entertain the non-drinker as they are in many other European countries – in particular Sweden. Although, as stated elsewhere in this book, the need for good non-alcoholic beverages is increasing all the time, if only for those who have to drive home, the market is not ready to fill this need. Doing the necessary research for the British edition of this book has proved illuminating. It is extremely hard to find a slightly wet drink in this country. Remember – it cannot be repeated too often – that these drinks do contain enough alcohol to be potentially upsetting, if not actually dangerous, to a recovering alcoholic. However it is useful to have alternatives to serve when you entertain people who, for one reason or another, prefer to imbibe less alcohol.

We have only been able to discover one brand of so-called 'alcohol-free' beer, *St. Christopher*. The label says 'not more than .05% alcohol which makes it an acceptable, slightly wet drink. Available at *The Victoria Wine Company*.

Leisure Drinks (see Appendix for their address) is a firm in Derbyshire which sells non-alcoholic (or de-alcoholized) drinks directly, by mail order. They have quite a large selection including:

Jung's   Alcohol-Free White Wine, medium dry, still
Alcohol-Free White Wine, extra dry, still
Alcohol-Free Red Wine, medium dry, still
Alcohol-Free Rosé Wine, medium dry, still
'Schloss Boosenburg', Alcohol-Free champagne style wine, sparkling.

The firm of *Carl Jung* was granted a patent to produce de-alcoholized wines as long ago as 1908 and has been doing so ever since. Their wines are made from grapes grown in the Rhine area of Germany. It is hoped that these wines will soon be available in supermarkets and through a large chain of wine merchants. In the meantime contact the distributors.

Also obtainable from *Leisure Drinks* are the following alcohol-free apéritifs, together with a very interesting and useful book by Anne Jesper entitled *Non-Alcoholic Cocktails:*

1. *Taki, Taki.* Resembles Bloody Mary
2. *Kas Bitter de Luxe.* From Spain, similar to Campari
3. *Palermo.* From France, serve like Vermouth
4. *Blancart Pastis.* From France. Aniseed flavour, like Pernod
5. *Jung's Vermouth.* Serve like Martini or mix.

Some branches of *The Victoria Wine Company* stock the following low-alcohol drinks:

St. Christopher Alcohol-free beer
Wunderbar   Rhine-type Red Wine, medium dry
              Rhine-type White Wine, medium dry
White Wedding, champagne-style wine, sparkling

If you have difficulty locating the wines, they can be ordered direct from the sole distributors in this country, Frank Wright Monday (for their address see Appendix).

Low alcohol-content beverages such as wine spritzers are not included in this book because they are regarded as ordinary alcoholic beverages that contain regulation amounts of alcohol and are merely diluted with water or fruit juice; they therefore do not qualify for inclusion here. The average wine spritzer contains in excess of .05% alcohol and tends to be mixed at a party to contain considerably more.

The Best of the Nondrinker's Favourites in Australia

In Australia, de-alcoholized wines (average .05% alcohol) are a booming market and there are quite a few brand names available throughout the country which are listed below. If you have difficulty finding any of them, there is a list of manufacturers in the Appendix.

Robinvale –   Burgundy-style red, medium dry
                Chablis, white, medium dry

Kaiser Stuhl –   white, still
                   champagne-style, sparkling

Chateau Yaldara –   Moselle-style white, still
                      Riesling-style, medium-dry
                      Lambrusco, red, sparkling
                      Spumante, white, sparkling
San Bernadino –   Gold Coast Chablis, Surf Cooler
Malva –   red, dry
            white, dry
            Port, ruby
Castella –   Sparkling White
               Spumante
               Lambrusco, red sparkling
               Rosé

In Australia there does not appear to be any truly non-alcoholic beer available i.e. (.05% or less.) The authorities have had little success when it comes to labelling non-alcoholic beers or 'brewed soft drinks' as they are called in Australia. The problem is that, generally, any brewed drink containing less than 1.5% alcohol can be labelled a 'brewed soft drink' and sold to any child in a supermarket. To add insult to injury other brewed drinks, labelled 'low alcohol beer', can actually have a much lower alcohol content than the so-called brewed soft drinks but must be sold through licensed liquor outlets.

   Most of the manufacturers of 'brewed soft drinks' were unable or unwilling to supply the exact alcohol content of their product. 'About 1% . . . or slightly less . . . or slightly more' was a fairly standard response. Of course, this complies with the law and puts their product in the category of a 'brewed soft drink'. However, when you're entertaining reformed drinkers or friends who simply want to get off the stuff '1% more or less' is frankly too much alcohol.

Queensland does seem to be leading the way and has recently introduced legislation prohibiting anything called a 'brewed soft drink' from containing more than .5% alcohol. This has meant that Queensland drink manufacturers have had to lower their alcohol content considerably to live with the new law. The present situation is so confused that we are, alas, unable to offer any helpful suggestions for Australian non-drinkers who have a taste for hops. If we have inadvertently overlooked any truly non-alcoholic beer please let us know (care of the publishers) and the information will be included in future editions.

Teas and Coffees

The endless varieties of tea and coffee available make it virtually impossible to reach any sort of consensus as to which ones are best. Therefore, beyond suggesting that you consider any ordinary blend (Indian or China) such as *Darjeeling, Orange Pekoe, Ceylon, Earl Grey* or *Lapsang Suchong* for breakfast and tea (for at least one of the teas served) we have no specific suggestions.

If you are a recovering alcoholic, you should examine the list of contents of the herbal teas to be sure that they contain no sedative herbs that might cause problems. An example: skullcap has a sedative effect that can be dangerous to a recovering alcoholic. If you find something unfamiliar on the ingredient list, check it out before drinking.

Iced tea, a delicious beverage not served often enough here, can be used as a base for any number of variations, both as 'cocktails' and for drinking with meals. Served with lemon, sugar, and fresh mint leaves, it makes a lovely (and innocuous) version of the dangerous mint julep.

Michelle Anderson, owner of a popular restaurant in the U.S. called 'Capers', is constantly asked for her recipe for Capers' famed Spiced Tea. Although she understandably prefers not to disclose the precise amounts involved, she graciously listed the ingredients for us: ordinary Indian tea, freshly made orange and lemon juice, cinnamon, and cloves. We suggest you experiment with this combination; if you come even close to the Capers' version, you will have a delicious drink indeed.

Coffee is an important topic to most nondrinkers, and even those who prefer to (or must) avoid caffeine tend to have definite views about decaffeinated varieties.

Simply stated, coffee comes in two basic types: 'light roasts,' which means that the beans have been roasted a short time, and 'dark roasts,' which describes beans that have been roasted longer and have a stronger flavour. Most supermarket blends are light roasts. Dark roasts deepen in intensity from dark brown Viennese to French Roast to Espresso which, when finely powdered, is called Turkish Roast.

The names of the seemingly endless number of blends vary according to the country of origin, roast, method of preparation, and the imagination of those who wish to entice the prospective purchaser by offering glorious visions of the ultimate cup of coffee. Coffee speciality shops provide inviting settings for devising your very own preferred combinations for special times of day, special occasions, and special people.

Whatever the blend, there are three crucial elements in correct coffee-making:

Crucial Element Number One: An utterly clean coffee pot. All surfaces must be sparkling and free of coffee oils, which cannot be dissolved by rinsing alone—serious scrubbing with soap, water, and elbow grease is required. Because leftover stains can pollute successive brews, it is essential to thoroughly clean the pot after each use.

Crucial Element Number Two: Coffee should never be prepared over a direct heat. If it boils, coffee instantly loses its flavour. So always make in a jug, cafetière, or by the filter or cona method. If the cona method is used you must resist the urge to 'keep it warm' on the stove. It will overheat and taste terrible.

Crucial Element Number Three: The coffee, to be at its peak, must be served immediately. Freshly brewed coffee, expecially the lighter roasts, sours quickly when left to sit, unless it's off the heat. But reheating can make it worse, and no, you shouldn't add water to it, and double no, you shouldn't run it through the already-used grounds. (The silver lining for dead coffee: turn it into iced coffee, which is virtually a whole new drink. Leftover coffee suffers almost not at all from refrigeration, and you can even keep adding it to whatever's already in the container in the fridge as the cold temperature maintains the flavour at a decidedly acceptable level.) A slight caveat here about serving intervals—brewed dark-roasted coffees can survive holding patterns best because they've had more roasting, which cuts the acidity; this extra roasting also makes them better candidates for reheating.

Other hints from my friend the coffee expert: Refrigerate your coffee beans or ground coffee in a tight container to maintain freshness. And serve milk or half cream-half milk to complement light-roasted coffee. Cream—light or heavy—tends to go better with dark-roasted and/or strong coffee.

Other Beverages

Hot cocoa, or the richer hot chocolate, can be inspired endings for a nonalcoholic meal. If you make it rich enough and provide a rich topping you can skip serving dessert, if you dare.

Your favourite fruit juice will taste better with food if you make it into a fruit juice spritzer. My personal favourite is cranberry juice cocktail★ with soda water. Blackberry Juice spritzer is also an excellent accompanying beverage. (*Lindavia* Blackberry Nectar is available in Health Food Shops)

You can make particularly attractive drinks by layering ingredients for a sunrise effect. Blackcurrant juice on the bottom, orange juice in the middle, soda water on top—yum. Don't let complicated cocktail recipes defeat you—just substitute the fruit juice for the alcohol, or simply prepare the mix without the booze.

Blender drinks made with fruit juice, fresh fruit, shaved ice, and soda water are excellent. Just remember that if you prepare these for recovering alcoholics, use a separate blender container from the one you're using for alcoholic drinks or rinse it carefully between batches.

Throughout the menu section there are general suggestions for complementary beverages. We hope that these will inspire you to try your hand at creating original concoctions of your own.

★ Available in larger supermarkets.

CHAPTER FOUR

Practical Substitutions and Alterations

Removing the Spirits Without Removing the Spirit

I'd like to take a minute here to talk a little about sauces. Virtually every cookery book is full of good sauce recipes, most of which do not contain alcohol. Sauce recipes that do contain alcohol can in many cases be made perfectly well without it. The sauces included here are those traditionally thought to 'require' the alcoholic ingredient that has become identified as an integral part of them. What we've done is to track down substitutes that will produce the texture and flavour of the original sauce without mimicking its alcoholic taste.

The easiest thing to do when you're confronted with making a nonalcoholic sauce from an alcohol-laden recipe is to think what else might be used instead. Any dessert sauce that has a teaspoon or tablespoon of alcohol or liqueur added can survive very nicely if you substitute something sweet and syrupy that has the same basic flavour. Curacao, Grand Marnier, and Cointreau are all orange-flavoured liqueurs and can be replaced by either orange syrup or a combination of orange syrup and grated orange rind, which gives the result a little sharper flavour (more like the Curacao), or frozen orange juice concentrate. Use exactly the same quantity that is called for in the recipe so that you don't run the risk of diluting the sauce.

The French use what they call 'Sirop de Fruits' to make drinks rather like our squashes but which are far tastier and more concentrated. These syrups come in a variety of flavours and are now widely available in this country. They are extremely useful substitutes for liqueurs in dessert sauces.

A recipe that calls for Framboise can be made instead with unsweetened raspberry juice, made by pressing fresh (or thawed unsweetened frozen) fruit through a sieve. It changes the colour of the sauce, of course, as the Framboise is clear, but you still get that nice raspberry flavour. If you need a stronger flavour, you can simmer the raspberry juice for a few minutes. Taste the juice as it evaporates and remove from heat when the flavour has reached the intensity you like. Freeze any extra for future use.

Much of the following material will appear in the various recipe sections, but a summary of this technique may help you with other recipes that you'd like to prepare without alcohol.

You can often adjust a recipe simply by leaving out the

ORANGE LIQUEURS

alcoholic ingredient and proceeding with the rest of the recipe as is. But this absolutely won't work when the volume added by the alcoholic ingredient must be replaced with a like amount of volume. In these cases, you must decide what to substitute for the alcoholic ingredient.

Desserts are usually very easy to work with; if a liqueur is required, it is relatively simple to substitute a fruit syrup of the same flavour as the liqueur. If syrup is not appropriate for the recipe, concentrated frozen juice often is, and if that won't do, you may be able to use plain juice, or make your own to provide unsweetened flavour.

What to Use in Place of . . .

Here are a few of the most practical substitutions:

Dark Rum—use dark syrup in the same quantity unless this amount is likely to create a sugary taste. Reduce the quantity of syrup if equal substitution will make the dish too sweet.

Light Rum—golden syrup.

Cognac—fresh apple juice laced with dark brown sugar. Use about a tablespoon of sugar to 100ml/¼ pint juice.

Curacao, Grand Marnier, or Cointreau—frozen concentrated orange juice. For Curacao add grated orange peel; about 1 teaspoon to 50ml/2 fl oz of concentrate.

Vanilla—see 'The Vanilla Dilemma,' our special section on vanilla.

Orange Extract—1 tablespoon grated orange peel, plus the oil obtained from bending the orange skin over the dish so the oil squirts into the dish. Keep this up until you have nice strong taste. Or use 1 tablespoon dried orange peel.

Lemon Extract—same process as for orange. Be careful with the amount you use—freshly grated lemon peel and oil can be very strong and may make the dish too bitter if you use too much. Substitute exactly ¼ teaspoon of rind for ¼ teaspoon of extract or use ¼ teaspoon dried lemon peel.

Almond Extract—use ground almonds in place of some of the flour, or use marzipan in place of some of the fat. Note: this will give a smooth sauce a grainy texture. To give an almond taste to a pie, use the almond in the pastry, put vanilla sugar in the filling, and omit the almond extract.

Sometimes you must come up with a totally different taste that will still complement the dish. For example, it took a lot of experimenting to find a substitute we liked for marsala in zabaglione or sherry in trifle. We finally arrived at frozen concentrated orange juice, which works very well in both cases. Old fashioned cream soda would work with the trifle as well.

When we began working on non-sweet dishes, we found that different solutions were in order. Here are some of the substitutions that work for us:

White Wine—depending on what you are cooking,

substitute an equal volume of chicken stock or fish stock (court bouillon). If the dish is strongly flavoured in other ways, you can also use water or a little cider vinegar with stock.

Red Wine—my favourite is a mixture of consommé and tomato juice or tomato-based vegetable juice. Don't use tomato soup as it is sweet and gets sweeter with hours of cooking. Neither do we recommend the spiced tomato mixers as they can be bitter and the spices can disflavour the rest of the recipe.

Framboise—unsweetened raspberry juice. Note: the juice will colour the dish, so review the other ingredients to be sure that you don't end up with a muddy, unappetizing colour.

Calvados or Cider—equal amount of fresh still apple juice. Calvados is a little sweet anyway, and is often used with chicken, which can easily stand the slight sweetness of apple juice. Do not use in quantities greater than 50 ml/2 fl oz as it will be too sweet.

Sherry—in a non-sweet recipe with some butter or oil among the ingredients, substitute 1 tablespoon of grapeseed oil for an equal amount of fat.

Brandy—'burnt' sugar. This is white sugar melted slowly in a heavy pan until it becomes a dark caramel colour. As it darkens, it will lose much of its sweetness, but you must stop before it gets too dark and begins to scorch. Take off heat when it's the right colour, cool slightly, and add an equal amount of water, drop by drop at first as it may splatter on the hot sugar. Store, tightly covered, in the refrigerator. If crystals form, open container or loosen top and set in a pan of hot water to dissolve them. Do not use more than 1 tablespoon.

There is some controversy about the use of various kinds of vinegar. Although there is no alcohol whatsoever in either red wine or white wine vinegar, I have friends who prefer not to use them. When I'm cooking for one of these friends I substitute plain, distilled malt vinegar for any recipe that calls for white wine vinegar, and raspberry vinegar* for red wine vinegar if it seems to me that the recipe will stand for it. Occasionally I'll substitute an apple cider vinegar.

Vinegar—white wine, use white distilled. Red wine, use raspberry vinegar or cider vinegar.

Cassis—*Lindavia* blackberry nectar (or, if you want unsweetened, make your own by pressing the fruit through a sieve. Freeze any extra for future use.)

* Available in larger supermarkets

Poaching Liquids

Because the enormous (and growing) number of different fish now available would require an equivalent array of fish recipes, let's focus instead on the one method of fish preparation that invariably calls for wine: Poaching. You have many choices for substitutions here, all of which will be governed by the kind of taste you want to end up with.

The simplest of all poaching liquids is plain, salted water, although it's not one I especially favour. What I like to do is to use homemade fish stock. It would never occur to me to poach a fish 'naked'; I always include some cut-up celery, carrot, and onion, and sometimes a bay leaf or a bit of special herb blend for fish in the poaching liquid. These are particularly useful additions if you plan to use the liquid later to make any type of sauce. Another trick is to remember to lightly butter or grease the poaching tray so that you won't have any trouble sliding the fish off. Using these wine-free stocks, you can proceed to use virtually anyone's recipe for poaching a particular kind of fish. Once you have poached the fish it's quite useful to reduce the poaching liquid, by boiling it down to about half of its original volume, and freeze it into ice cubes for storage. These will give you a much fresher flavour than will commercial fish bouillon cubes.

Braising Liquid For Meat and Poultry

A general note about stewing and braising: here again many recipes will call for some kind of wine. My substitution for white wine is an equal amount of chicken stock that includes a small amount of tomato juice. If the recipe calls for 900 ml/1½ pints of white wine, you would substitute a total of 900ml/1½ pints of chicken stock or stock/tomato juice mixed. If you want to keep the sauce completely white, put in 900ml/1½ pints of chicken stock or, if the stock is thick, 450ml/¾ pint of chicken stock and 300ml/½ pint of tomato juice; if you want it darker yet add a tablespoon or so of tomato paste. If the recipe already calls for stock as well as wine, increase the stock to equal the quantity required by *both* the wine *and* the stock *less* 300 ml/½ pint and then decide whether you want to add either tomato paste or the same amount of tomato juice. Avoid prepared tomato sauces because they tend to be too heavy and not what we're looking for in this kind of recipe. Remember that whenever you add tomato to a sauce that contains nothing but white wine the resulting colour will be different from the original.

If a recipe calls for something sweet, like a Madeira or Port, there are a number of fairly exotic fruit juices that can be substituted in small quantities. For instance, blackcurrant juice can stand in for Port nicely as it's not too sweet. A visit to the local health food shop to check out the juices they have available can really be inspirational in this cooking approach. Meats such as pork, duck, and ham are quite happy with a slightly sweet sauce. Remember, too, that if the sauce calls for Madeira or Port to begin with it already hints at sweetness. When fruit juice is added in place of alcohol you must cut the amount in half to offset the intensity and sweetness of the juice. Make up the rest of the volume with either stock, cooking liquid, or water.

To give a little kick to a sauce that calls for cognac, try a teaspoon or so of a smooth Dijon mustard prepared without white wine.

Calvados or cider sometimes appear in cream sauces for chicken. A good substitute in this case is one of the French ciders that contain no alcohol, or a fresh apple juice. Again, you'll want to cut the amount back a bit because the unfermented apple juice will be sweeter than the Calvados. In order to retain the apple flavour, you can sometimes add slices of apple to cook with the meat, removing them before the sauce is made.

Remember, whether you entertain recovering alcoholics or other nondrinkers, are a recovering alcoholic yourself, or simply prefer to abstain from alcohol in any form, avoid both the so-called nonalcoholic beer and de-alcoholized wine. De-alcoholized wine, as we have noted, contains up to .05 percent alcohol and so does 'non-alcoholic' beer. To give you an idea of the dangers for recovering alcoholics, ordinary shandy contains 1.2% alcohol.

CHAPTER FIVE

Entertaining

The Cocktail Party, Large and Small

I can now, at this stage of my life, candidly confess to all my lovely and loving friends that cocktail parties are my least favourite events. Standing about with a dripping glass in my hand has never appealed to me, and I never could figure out how to hold anything else while balancing a drink and trying to shout over the background noise.

Giving the cocktail party is something else, however. (Believe me, gang, I *love* to give them, I do, I do! Don't go away!)

The term 'cocktail' is variously defined as:

any of an assortment of short mixed drinks;
a portion of prawns, crabmeat, shrimp, lobster, or the like served with a sauce;
a mixture of chilled cut fruits;

New do's and don'ts

Traditional cocktail parties feature an open bar, mostly alcoholic drinks, and savoury foods. Dedicated drinkers tend to favour nuts and other 'nibbles'. Their less-determined counterparts tend to explore the hot and cold hors d'oeuvres. Often these self-conscious efforts at providing relaxation are business gatherings; more often they are staged by friends after work or at the weekend.

Two bars: wet and dry

If you enjoy giving early-evening cocktail parties and want to make your nondrinking guests feel at ease, it is only necessary to provide a bar offering nonalcoholic beverages in addition to the one that offers alcohol. You may even include the nuts 'n nibbles.

Exotic blender drinks that are gulped with delight and without booze should—better make that *must*—have a separate blender at the dry bar for the very reason that they are gulped so readily. Reason one, the obvious: you can't use the same blender for both types of drinks because traces of alcohol would remain in the blender. Reason two, the not-obvious-until-too-late: the drinker who becomes a wild 'n crazy gulper because he thinks there ain't no alcohol in it—that it's a dry softee—may get the real thing in the same blender and become a wild 'n crazy guy ready for a laugh or an ambulance, depending on the circumstances.

Easier to provide on the dry bar are the more-and-more popular carbonated fruit juices that are packaged to look like wine and are good even without lowering the lights and raising the music.

Remember to provide separate glasses for the two bars. When you have ten or twelve people in for cocktails you shouldn't have any trouble keeping these things separate, but if you plan to invite a larger group, better look in on the chapter dealing with that Big Saturday Night Party for tips on how to keep the imbibers and abstainers on separate tracks.

If yours is a minimalist approach and you only want a brief affair in consideration of dinner somewhere else, then you might simply offer honey-roasted nuts along with the salted and unsalted mixed varieties as well as a small assortment of raw vegetables. Biscuits should include the slightly sweet digestive type as well as the unsweetened ones. Sweet cheeses, such as cream cheese, are a treat alongside the serious ones. Save the wine cheddar and other cheese spreads with alcohol content for another day or identify them so your nondrinking guests won't get some by mistake.

So-called 'alcohol-removed' wine and 'nonalcoholic' beer go on the wet bar. These beverages are sometimes imposters in that they contain small amounts of alcohol which a recovering alcoholic can't drink. Anyway, they taste very much like the real stuff, which is what these guests are intentionally avoiding.

When you extend the invitation, it is wise to state the exact hours, say from 5.30 to 7.30 p.m. This will act as a definite signal to your guests that it will not be dinner. If your party is without alcohol altogether and you're not sure of your guests' preferences, then note clearly but discreetly on the invitation, 'Alcoholic beverages will not be served.' (This avoids guests being surprise-surprised at the door, which can be grim for the dependent alcoholic. Few things are more depressing to certain guests

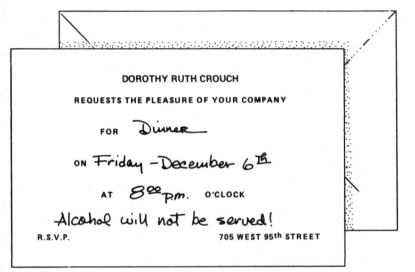

DOROTHY RUTH CROUCH

REQUESTS THE PLEASURE OF YOUR COMPANY

FOR Dinner

ON Friday - December 6th

AT 8ºº p.m.   O'CLOCK

Alcohol will not be served!

R.S.V.P.   705 WEST 95th STREET

anticipating intoxication for relaxation than to find out the drinks are minus the booze.) Alcohol-free cocktail parties make life a lot easier for you and your guests. You need have only one bar, your food need only complement the nonalcoholic beverages, and you don't have to patrol the area slapping the wrists of those using the wrong glasses.

Seriously, I strongly encourage you to try this kind of event if it is new to you. Not only are people just as lively when they're not drinking, they stay that way. Give the food the chance to supply the high and you'll discover your guests can sustain energy for the party at full tilt until the appointed hour when they depart in both good cheer and good health.

Perhaps instead of a cocktail party, you might want to give a real tea party at the same hour of the day. The problem with a cocktail party from my point of view is that it was created to propel people into drinking in order to 'unwind' and is therefore automatically tipped (no pun intended) in favour of the drinker. The tea party favours the nondrinker and provides a nice range of food, which can be perfect as a late afternoon pick-me-up. You can always have a small bar with alcoholic beverages at a teaparty to keep your drinkers happy and 'unwound' their way. Don't be concerned about your non-drinkers. They are sure to dive into the tea, coffee, and comestibles. There are no glasses to segregate, just cups for everything except the alcoholic drinks.

The Tea in all its Glory

And then there always is, shall always be, the good old traditional afternoon 'Tea,' when people steep, sip, and exchange the latest gossip without the twist of booze.

Few guests really expect to booze it up at tea. If the event is being held for business purposes you will already have announced the news ahead of time—dampening to some, of little moment to most—that alcohol will not be served, so your guests will know what to expect. The business-boozer can always order a drink on an emergency basis of allergy to tea, coffee, or even to—the unthinkable—hot chocolate.

Note also that a proper tea, with its delicious refreshments, affords nutrition at the time of day when it is most needed, in contrast to the artificial high induced by junk snacks and spirits.

Teatime usually extends from 4 to 6 p.m. the beginning—for better or for worse—of the cocktail hour for those who will be dining early. One way around this is to serve what's known as 'high' tea (for which my Uncle Harry again has his own definition) which includes more food than teas designed to fuel folks through until supper.

For the moment, however, let us simply serve tea. Much is being written, incidentally, about the 'Power Tea,' which appears to be another sign of the less-alcoholic times. Many people seem to be losing interest in drinking after working a full day, preferring to devote their evening to more rewarding pastimes.

The two most common kinds of traditional teas are 'Afternoon Tea' and 'Cream Tea.' Afternoon Tea always includes sandwiches made with cold sliced meat as well as the usual salad garnishes and sweets. Depending on the size of the group, let's say from one to nine, several kinds of tea may be served; sometimes coffee is served as well. In this country work is frequently interrupted at 3.30 or 4 p.m. while everyone has a cup of tea and a biscuit.

Why not include sparkling water and soft drinks as well as tea? Many people enjoy a cold drink in the afternoon and teatime comes at just the right hour.

As for food, the traditional range is so vast that there is sure to be something for everyone.

In a very small group (two to six people), the hostess or host pours unless someone else volunteers to be 'mother', a custom handed down to us by tradition. Usually the honour falls to the Senior Woman in the party (if one can be found); however, anyone in the group can muddle through the process regardless of age.

Tea is served in one pot, hot water in a second pot, with milk, sugar, and lemon on the side. In a formal service there is a special pot covered with lattice work (a bit like a street grate) for the 'slops' (these are not, as Uncle Harry contends, certain unwelcome guests). Slops are the small amounts of tea left in the bottom of the cup which, because they have become lukewarm, are poured out before the second cup of tea.

There are various methods of pouring, the most usual being to pour the tea into the cup, stopping in time to leave space for additional hot water for those who prefer a lighter brew. (Some tea aficionados like truly potent brews—what an Irish acquaintance calls 'trotting-mouse' tea.) Once this is added, the recipient is offered sugar, lemon, or milk. (Cream is a never-never with tea as it creates a greasy residue on top; this can spoil both the appearance of the tea and the appetite of the guest.) The person pouring continues round and about the circle to each of the guests, who keep their same cups for the duration of the event.

Food at an informal gathering is usually put on a tray so that individuals can help themselves, and each person is provided with a plate, napkin, and sometimes a knife. You will need a knife for a Cream Tea, which must have—are you keeping up with me?—hot scones with clotted cream and jam for the scones (or other hot rolls, if you insist), sometimes with butter as well as jam.

After everyone has a cup of tea, the guests are asked to help themselves to the sandwiches; the breads and cakes await the second service. The general idea here is to let everyone satisfy their late-day hunger pangs. The sandwiches suggested will stave off your guests' afternoon crankiness as they prepare for the plunge into the delectable sweets to come.

Here are some menu ideas for tea:

Afternoon Tea, English Style

Serve sandwiches made with sliced boiled ham, smoked salmon, cucumber, sliced egg, sliced chicken, watercress. (*Note:* English tea sandwiches are prepared by removing the crusts from thinly sliced white and whole wheat bread. Both sides are then lightly coated with butter, and a slice of meat or a thin layer of sliced egg or peeled cucumber is placed between the buttered slices. If you wish to include lettuce, select the flattest, thinnest leaf. Cut each sandwich into four pieces, either diagonally or lengthwise into fingers.)

At least one really super-gooey cake is absolutely essential to a proper tea, which should also include a sponge cake or lightly iced cake, some plain biscuits, and perhaps a pastry or two.

The Cream Tea, Australian Style

Serve hot scones, with or without raisins.

Honey

Fruit jams

Whipped cream, slightly sweetened if you like, but with no vanilla essence added

A good black tea like English Breakfast, Prince of Wales, or Ceylon Breakfast. Some people favour Earl Grey or Orange Pekoe, but I personally don't like the combination for a Cream Tea.

High Tea, American Style

Serve sandwiches made with sliced smoked ham, sliced roast beef, egg mayonnaise, chicken mayonnaise, cream cheese with olive or pimento.

Garnish with cherry tomatoes, lettuce, green olives.

Sweets can include miniature brownies, butterscotch brownies, date bars, Parisian Waffles.*

Serve any of the Indian Teas, including the Darjeeling and Assam.

Tea can encompass a business engagement and be served for you at a nearby tearoom. To find a place nearby, inquire at local hotels, particularly if you live in an urban area, and traditional lunch places if you live in a less populated area. Many restaurants and cafés that do not have bars serve hearty fare and by 4 p.m. are ready for tea. These same establishments can be excellent sources of food if you decide to have tea sent in.

You might also bring the necessary ingredients to the office and make your appointment for 4 p.m. or so. My preference for an office tea is often based on paper plates and plastic cups (shocking, I know, but so sensible). Tea (or coffee) can be served with a minimum of clean-up mess. At these informal events it's acceptable

* Recipes included

to forgo the sandwiches and merrily go for the sweets —some kind of very good biscuits or small pastries from the baker. Using paper cups and staging the event in the office may help to avoid addressing the question of alcohol (notwithstanding the cunning resourcefulness of certain drinkers with a mission).

The New Power Tea

If the occasion is to be a power tea, it will be more effective held away from the office (unless you have the luxury of a spacious conference room), china service must be used, and you must be ready to serve an alcoholic beverage (if permitted by your company policy—some companies do not allow alcohol to be served on their premises).

To sum up: Tea is now 'in,' and cocktails have become passé in many areas.

Brunch: The New Cocktail Hour?

In recent years, brunch seems to have become the most alcoholic meal of the day. There you are, absolutely starving, it's 12.30 or 1 p.m. and on come the Bloody Mary's, the Screwdrivers, the Mimosas, and so on. By the time you get through an average brunch, you may have to sleep through what's left of the afternoon before you're able to finish reading the Sunday paper. From the point of view of the guest who doesn't drink, brunch can be an uneasy prospect even at a restaurant, since alcohol is tucked into so many corners of the menu.

If you'd like to serve brunch to both drinkers and nondrinkers, you might consider a champagne brunch, with alcohol served as a drink rather than hidden in a Bloody Mary or in coffee or orange juice. Plain champagne can be served separately, with orange, grapefruit, or tomato juice *au naturel* available for abstainers. The menu can encompass any number of traditional and/or continental dishes *sans* alcohol. Fortunately most brunch dishes are usually made without alcohol and it's very easy to avoid it in sauces, gravies, and other such dressings. Serve the champagne in champagne glasses or wine glasses and the fruit juices in fruit juice glasses so that there can be no confusion. I would skip apple juice at this occasion since it's almost the same colour as champagne. A nice touch: fruit juice diluted with soda water to make a kind of fruit spritzer. These can be exhilarating in the morning and even more appealing when spruced up with mint or strawberries.

Plan to announce a definite time for eating to begin so that your nondrinking friends don't become cross-eyed on the highly sugared fruit juice before getting solid food. Along with such appetizers as cheese and raw vegetables, you might serve bite-size Danish or other pastries. Within half an hour of the guests' arrival, be ready for the food to begin. In addition to champagne, sparkling fruit juice, and ordinary fruit juice, plan to keep the coffee and tea flowing throughout the meal rather than just at the end of it. You might also serve a variety of jams and honeys with the rolls or pastries that accompany the meal. Since you have a small group it isn't necessary to trouble over any kind of a bar for your drinkers. Simply set each place according to whether or not the person is drinking at that seat and arrange your glasses accordingly. Then throughout the meal you can easily replenish whatever people are drinking. Arrange your seating plan so that guests are in comfortable positions for lively conversation during brunch. If you are accustomed to traditional heavy-drinking brunches, you may be surprised by the spirited and merry chattering of a room full of people whose 'highs' are sparked solely by the food, sweet juices, and scrumptious pastries.

For those who prefer alcoholic beverages at brunch, I recommend that the drinks be light in alcohol. At this time of day empty stomachs can be highly susceptible to its effects.

Breakfast: When Drinks Are Not Expected

Some of the brunch menus in the menu section hark back to traditional breakfast-type menus and are thus appropriate to serve earlier in the day.

A word about breakfast: if you choose to serve breakfast rather than brunch, very few people will expect alcohol, which gives you the opportunity to have a big breakfast party without it. If you decide to start at, say, 9.30 or 10 o'clock in the morning as opposed to the 12 or 1 p.m. brunch hour (and have friends who are up at that hour), you could offer not only fruit juice at the start but coffee and tea from the very beginning. These would then be served throughout the meal. Whether it's breakfast or brunch, by the way, it's a very good idea to have plain sparkling mineral or soda water available during the entire meal. Fruit juice and either of the above, splashed together, often pleases young children more than soda-pop, and this is one of those meals where you should be prepared to accommodate children as well as adults. Because, alas, it's not likely that your guests can easily get someone to look after the children at that hour of the morning. Breakfast or brunch, if you want an 'adult' party even though children will be on hand, I think it's a welcome gesture to provide baby-sitting service in your home and to give the youngsters their own area in which to congregate and eat.

The 'older' ones, however, will not want to be relegated to the 'baby' room and you should be prepared with drinks like fruit juice spritzers for them at the table.

Lunch or Dinner

These are probably the easiest occasions at which to

entertain both drinking and nondrinking guests. Since everyone will be seated, you don't have to worry too much about someone getting the wrong drink. Still, there are a few precautions to be taken.

Timing

To begin with, set an exact time on the invitation for your meal, such as '7.30 for 8. p.m.' or 'You may arrive at 7.30 p.m. for dinner at 8,' or 'If you can't make it by 8, dinner is at 9,' or, more formally, 'Reception at 7 p.m. Service at 8 p.m.' This specifically limits the interval between arrival and seating and tactfully lets those who don't want to stand around (with or without conversational preliminaries) know when you plan to begin serving. A half-hour is the usual before-dinner interval and I normally allow a 15 minute nodding introduction pre-lunch on a weekday. Weekend lunches can easily occupy the full 30 minute conversational warm-up, and at Saturday night dinner an hour may be barely adequate for introducing guests who may a) hate each other, or b) end up marrying each other. (And maybe eventually divorcing, but that's for another Saturday night.)

When your guests arrive, offer them some refreshment, alcoholic or otherwise, until just before you are ready to seat them. At that point, don't offer late arrivals drinks as they will have no time to enjoy them. As on other occasions when you have drinkers and nondrinkers to entertain, keep the alcoholic drinks in glasses that are distinguishable by shape or code from the nonalcoholic drinks. It isn't necessary or particularly wise to offer snacks at this stage as it is preferable that guests avoid filling themselves up on hors d'oeuvres.

Seating

When the appointed hour arrives, lead your guests to the

table and usher them to their places. Don't wait too long for a real latecomer. Just leave that place empty and seat the guest unobtrusively when he or she arrives. (I don't believe in keeping the others waiting for more than a few minutes.) It is the host's prerogative to decide where the guests sit, and this privilege can be used strategically for general compatibility of personalities and ease of presence to ensure that an excellent time is had by all. (I try to seat my Uncle Harry away from women of any age or marital status.) Think about the individual qualities of your guests, what they like to talk about, how they like to eat, and specifically—given the focus of this book—whether or not they are drinkers. I usually scatter my nondrinkers around the table, pairing them conversationally rather than worrying about whether or not they are seated next to a drinker. The only exception is if I have a very heavy drinker or a still-drinking alcoholic at the table. Then I will probably locate that person where he or she will not be made to feel awkward by the guest/guests who don't drink.

Special Glasses for Special Guests

With prearranged seating, it is also easy to set the right kind of glass at each place, which then becomes a clue to the kind of drink to serve. I usually dispense wine, sparkling water, sparkling fruit juice, and plain iced water at a meal. Iced tea is a refreshing drink at most times of the year, but I am not personally fond of it in the winter.

If you have even one nondrinker as a lunch or dinner guest, your meal should not contain alcohol. Cooked-down wine sauces may have zero alcohol content but still conjure up bad times for a recovering alcoholic since an undertaste provides a stubborn reminder of the past. By the way, this does not have to be the recent past. I know people who haven't had anything alcoholic to drink for at least 20 years but are still susceptible to instantly recalling the taste and don't want it in food. There are too many good dishes that can be prepared without alcohol to rely on traditional alcohol-based sauces. Elegance can be conveyed by the use of your best tableware and napkins, and, most importantly, by careful presentation of the food. Against the background of formal style, the meal itself attains a fashionable aura. Those little parsley sprigs and similar garnishes go a long way toward making the meal a festive occasion.

Buffets—labels for the wary

When your table seats eight but you want to have twelve or fourteen people to dinner, the obvious solution is a buffet dinner. Convert your dining-room table for the buffet and make the coffee table the focal point of the meal. If the guests are to serve themselves beverages, you may want to refer to the sections on Brunch and the Big Saturday Night Party to see how to set up separate wet and dry bars; otherwise you can serve from the kitchen. Simply make sure that you have the glasses coded for alcohol/nonalcohol. Remember to include all of the falsely labelled 'alcohol-free' wine on the *alcoholic* beverage list so that you don't inadvertently serve it to a recovering alcoholic.

Order of service for a buffet, whether lunch or dinner, is very much the same as for a sit-down occasion except that you simply announce that lunch or dinner is served instead of leading your guests to the table. Make your announcement loudly and clearly if the buffet table and the party are all in the same room. Guests usually recognize an undisturbed platter and wait until the host/hostess gives the signal to begin disturbing it. (Except for Uncle Harry, who must inevitably be wrist-slapped into submission.) In a living/dining area, keep the pre-meal offerings (which are designed to be disturbed) on the coffee table away from the main table and there is likely to be no confusion.

Because people keep their glasses throughout the meal at a buffet, once the guests are given their nondrinking or drinking shape or colour of glass, you only have to keep refilling it with the chosen drink. If a guest switches from nonalcoholic to alcoholic in the middle of things, get the person a new glass for alcoholic drinking. The object is to avoid having alcoholic drinks in the nonalcoholic coded glasses so that there is no chance that a recovering alcoholic will pick up the glass and get a traumatic mouthful by mistake.

A sad but necessary warning: If you notice a recovering alcoholic guest suddenly using a 'drinker's glass,' remind him of it, but do so gently. He may have decided to take that drink, after all. It is his privilege because it is his decision. Only he can determine his alcoholic status, if one in fact exists. You may be witnessing a 'slip,' or you may not. After he replies (perhaps irritably, perhaps sadly) that the drink is indeed intended, then gently, very gently, indicate understanding—maybe with a smile or a nod—and gracefully offer your guest whatever drink desired. He is no longer an ex-drinker. Go on with your chores, then. It is time for restraining yourself and suppressing whatever you may feel about that person's choice. It is time for getting on with your party, and your guests are looking for you.

Food at a buffet should be planned so that you don't have to be stuck in the kitchen at the last minute preparing things. For this reason you often see dishes like beef burgundy and coq au vin on a buffet table. Except for the preliminaries, the whole meal requires only small plates for the first course and/or salad and dinner plates for the main course. For a smaller selection, dinner plates are enough. Since the group is larger than usual you may be straining your supply of china to supply two plates per guest. You'll then have to choose between washing plates between courses, serving dessert on paper plates, or selecting a finger-food dessert.

Remember, when you have drinking and nondrinking guests, not to dawdle over pre-dinner drinks and snacks. Plan no more than one hour for the preliminaries and then announce that dinner is being served. Latecomers at a buffet are not an imposition as there is no reason to hold up the action to wait for a late guest (unless it is a special occasion and the guest is the honoured person!).

At a big buffet you can serve a dish or two with alcohol-based sauces as long as you are willing to label them. I don't really like the idea of serving food that some can't eat, but it can be done with reasonable grace if you are offering a number of choices. (Why treat allergy to alcohol differently than allergy to, say, shellfish?) The difference is in knowing about it in advance so that you can adjust your menu accordingly. If you don't have this advance knowledge, you simply offer a normal variety of choices. There are many more people who are allergic to alcohol than there are people who are allergic to shellfish (or strawberries, or whatever), and your chances of encountering people with other serious food allergies are much less. Another difference: a guest with a serious food problem will warn you in advance, nothing-to-be-ashamed-of. Most people readily do—unless their allergy is to alcohol. Recovering alcoholics wait to manage the menace anonymously without drawing attention to themselves. We should understand and expect it. If the group is small, and includes one or two people you don't know well, inquire in advance about preferences, or else offer enough choices to avoid a problem.

After-Theatre Suppers—how to detour 'after-drinking' drivers

All the rules for buffet dinner also apply to after-theatre supper. Menus for the late supper are lighter and can be selected from brunch or lunch menus. Or instead of serving a whole supper late at night, offer guests dessert and coffee only. By desserting the event (pun! pun!) you have made it a basically nonalcoholic affair, much as you did when you exchanged the tea for the cocktail party. I prefer to eat something before an evening event and am always ready and willing for something after. A dessert is irresistible at around 10.30 or 11 p.m., with coffee and tea the main accompaniments along with espresso and cappucino and perhaps hot chocolate (see the beverage section for my answer to Irish coffee). If you have insistent drinkers, provide some champagne and brandy or a liqueur. As for the food itself, service is easier as you only need to supply one dish per guest and you need only forks and spoons. The motorists on their way home afterward will be especially happy about being given a choice. I would also have some decaffeinated coffee and tea on hand for those who don't sleep when they consume the real thing at that late hour.

If you live in a motoring community and a majority of your guests are driving, you might want to offer 'alcohol-removed' wine or champagne for a late-night supper. This would be a good choice for all *but* the recovering alcoholics, who can't have the .05 percent alcohol left in this kind of wine.

The Big Saturday Night Party

The day is fast approaching and you've just realized how many of your guests won't be drinking—or can't drink—alcohol. What to do? What do you serve these concerned motorists, recovering alcoholics, and those who abstain for religious or health reasons? Some of your guests, who do not enjoy the privilege of preference, will be bringing their special sensitivities to the least drop of alcohol. And now you're worried, because you love them.

Space Requirements—where to serve what

The first thing to do for your nondrinking guests is to check out your party space and begin to arrange for completely separate areas for two bars. One will be the usual one with alcoholic drinks, soft drinks, and lightly alcoholic drinks. The other will offer beverages that have no alcohol whatsoever. Make sure that the so-called 'nonalcoholic' drinks are nowhere near your dry bar. This whole new category of 'lightly' alcoholic drinks, upon close label inspection, reveals a startling one-to three-percent alcohol content. One of these can be as dangerous to a recovering alcoholic as a full-strength drink.

Next, supply glasses or cups of differing shapes or colours on the two bars. I have one friend who uses coloured plastic on the 'wet' bar and clear plastic on the 'dry' one. Another friend likes the squat water tumblers on the dry bar, reserving the stemmed wine glasses for the wet one. This could be important to ex-drinkers, who would rather not be reminded of their drinking days when they carried a few too many traditional alcohol-containing glasses. This is a large party, remember, and you won't have advance knowledge of each preference or sensitivity. So play it safe—avoid uneasy encounters with alcoholic mementoes on the dry bar.

Punch Bowls—to spike or not to spike

If you plan to serve punch in addition to individual drinks, you face another dilemma. To spike or not to spike: that is the question. You might consider two punch bowls (space allowing), one with alcohol and one without. Be sure to make the punches different colours. For example, you could serve a claret punch and a light strawberry punch, but the colours of a champagne and an apple juice or tea-based punch would be much too close for comfort. The spiked bowl should then be labelled 'wine punch' or 'rum punch' or something similar so that your non-drinkers can safely detour to the right libation. On the outside chance that there may be a joker or two in the crowd, it's a good idea to let arriving guests know that you have a bowl of unspiked punch and it's to stay that way. I once dealt with this matter by spreading the rumour that anyone who spiked my plain punch would never be invited back. It worked! (After tasting the plain one they wanted to come back even more.) Premixed drinks like mai-tais, screwdrivers, bloody Mary's and the like are best made without alcohol and placed on the dry bar. One need only take them to the wet bar to spike (and be spiked). It is very risky to have identical-looking mixtures around, some with alcohol and some without. To your ex-drinkers, facing undecipherable lookalikes is on a par with being a Roman Christian trying to decide which door has the lion behind it.

Basic Food Rules for Mixed Parties (Drinkers and Nondrinkers)

At a big party, food usually comes out of the kitchen in waves, beginning with cheese, biscuits, crisps and vegetables with dips, and rolling on through more substantial fare if the affair is a late one. Guests may bring gifts of food to serve at the party. There are two basic rules for food at a mixed party of drinkers and nondrinkers: 1) *it should be immediately and constantly available,* and 2) *there should be no alcohol in any of it.*

To take rule one first, people who don't drink are not interested in standing around for an hour or so before they get something to eat. Recovering alcoholics in particular have healthy appetites and look forward to the food. Several of them tell me that food is truly exciting now that they can taste it. Have plenty of it out from the very beginning of the party.

Rule two is also hard and fast—there should be no alcohol whatsoever in any of the food offered. You can control anything you make yourself. Specifically, alcohol is taboo in finishing sauces, such as devilled dishes, which are often complemented with brandy, and sauces that have been reduced may no longer contain alcohol, but will perpetuate the taste of their beginnings, such as the wine of beef burgundy or the beer taste present in Carbonnades à la Flamande. Many former drinkers loathe the disturbing taste of cooked alcohol in these sauces, and unless you know your guests very well, it's best to avoid them. Commercially prepared food must have ingredient labels; exceptions include paté or cheese that is purchased at a local gourmet shop and cut from a large loaf or wheel. Do suspect paté, as it often contains sherry or brandy or both. Ask the salesperson to show you the list of ingredients.

Beware of Guests Bearing Gifts

Food brought by guests presents no serving problems. If the gift is a brandied chicken liver spread, just whip out a blank card from your reserve supply, label it 'brandied chicken liver' and place it away from the main food table in the appropriate vicinity of the wet bar. You need not label anything without alcohol.

Question the cook to determine whether or not a label is required. *Caution of Cautions:* If you have a cook from the 'I-don't-trust-anyone-who-doesn't-drink' school, be incisive in your probe. There are also cooks who think 'a little bit won't hurt.' Question these individuals carefully. If you're worried that the cook may be insulted by one of your alcohol-alert cards, say 'oh, this looks too good to put out. I'm going to be greedy and save it for later,' or 'oh, how wonderful, you brought my favourite marinated marigolds. I'm not sharing this. Let's put it away and have it later.' I promise you, this works every time.

For Chocoholics and other Dessert Freaks: The Sweet Corner

One extra sign of your entertaining expertise that is much appreciated by nondrinkers at big, late parties is a sweet corner, which features an unending flow of coffee and hot water for various teas, coffees, and decaffeinated versions of both. This area should be either at one end of the savoury food line or set up in a separate nook. Unusual as it may seem, it should be available all evening, not just at the end. Providing this warm and refreshing niche makes it easier for your sober-for-the-night drivers to resist the thought of taking even one drink. Sugar can often induce as buoyant a feeling as alcohol, and really rich goodies keep the drivers from feeling deprived. After all, they aren't getting any alcohol calories, so they can go wild on the sweets. If you have a pet baba or rum cake that your drinkers are eagerly anticipating, just place it near the other alcohol-laced food and mark it well with a card. Keep the special sweet area 'dry.' Forget those artificial alcohol flavours— they're no-no's. A nondrinker often can't discriminate between rum and rum flavouring. Vanilla's not too bad if it has been cooked, as in a cake or cooked pudding. If not, it's wiser to stick with vanilla syrup or vanilla sugar, as discussed in 'The Vanilla Dilemma.' Desserts that usually contain alcohol can be enjoyed by your nondrinking guests if you prepare them by using flavours that do not mimic the original alcoholic taste, as described in the dessert section of this book.

My shaky first try at a big, mixed party found me thoroughly confused by all the separate areas required by my nondrinking guests. To help you avoid the pre-party jitters, here is a description of the items contained in each of the separate areas and a floor plan of a typical kitchen-living-room-dining area combination showing details of location.

Wet Bar: Set it up near the alcohol and wines (unless

you are concerned that heavy drinkers may invade your special bottles). It will house whisky, vodka, gin, rum, red and white wine, beer, low-alcohol beer, low-alcohol cider, tonic, soda water, sodium-free mineral water, (in consideration of your friends who must watch their salt intake), colas, diet sodas, and ginger ale; various bar fruits such as sliced lemon, lime, and maraschino cherries; olives and cocktail onions; ice; cups or glasses coded for the wet bar; and napkins.

Dry Bar: Set this up across the room from the wet bar, or at the other end of the counter. (You may not want to have people passing the wet bar to reach the dry one.) Here you display mineral water, tonic or soda water, diet sodas, several flavours of regular fizzy drinks, such as ginger ale or bitter lemon, fruit juice (orange, tomato, lemonade, apple), sparkling fruit juice; various citrus fruits (sliced lemon, lime, or orange): cups or glasses coded for the dry bar; and napkins. I like the idea of using separately shaped tumblers to prevent accidents, as I have already mentioned.

Punch Bowl(s): Punch is optional, but is also fun. If you have two bowls, put 'em at opposite ends of the main food table. The cups or glasses echo the code used on the wet and dry bars, and you might also code the napkins. Each bowl goes at its separate end of the table, clearly designated spiked or not by its entourage of coded glasses and napkins and the presence of a sign if spiked.

Food without alcohol occupies the main dining room table and the coffee table in the sitting room, if you have one. Keep it at a respectful distance from the wet bar.

Food containing alcohol is placed as accessibly near the wet bar as possible. If this bar is on the counter, the booze-laden food surrounds it. Hint from the experienced: be sure to supply extra plates near this area so that guests can load up there and then and not move them by mistake to the main food areas. Since we've agreed that all foods containing alcohol are labelled, provide yourself with blank labels in a handy place so that you can be quick on the draw to brand any gift foods that arrive unexpectedly during the party.

Coffee, tea, and nonalcoholic sweets: These warming things of life need a place by themselves. If you are not serving punch or are having only one bowl, this set-up can go at one end of the main food table. Otherwise it does very well on a card table. If you are using a large coffee-maker, you'll want to place the table near an electric socket and keep a coffee warmer or warmer tray handy. (You may prefer to locate this table so that guests need not pass close to the wet bar to reach it.)

Diagram of Room Arrangements

The accompanying diagram is based on a typical apartment with no formal dining room. Guests habitually wander in and out of the kitchen, hall, and living room with its dining area. It is not meant as a typical example of how to use space for a mixed party since the space available is considerably smaller than that of most houses.

If you have more space to spread out in, be sure you don't distance your drinkers and nondrinkers on separate floors or so far away that they may never see each other again. If this is unavoidable, put the wet bar and alcohol-laden food in the less accessible place. Drinkers are resourceful and relentless and will find the bar wherever you put it, thence to cheerfully return to mingle at the main food table.

Depending on your guests' attractions to each other, your party may be a late one. Be prepared, like the good scout you of course are, by making sure you have plenty of food on hand and that you will be ready to serve the cheery throng again at midnight and even thereafter.

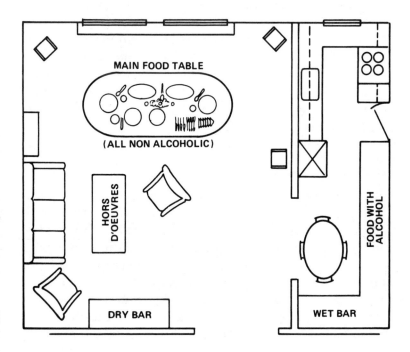

Keeping the Whole Party Dry

Another major option for your party is to choose to keep the whole affair dry. This decision works surprisingly well if you let the guests know at the time you extend the invitation that there will be no alcohol served. At the same time, you can let prospective guests know that bottles of alcohol brought to the party won't be served. Many people have reduced their intake of alcohol for a variety of reasons, and are just as happy without it as with it. If you choose to have a dry party, increase the amount of food you would normally supply by about one-third. Do keep the coffee/tea and cake corner going all evening—believe me—and have fun preparing the richest possible sweet dishes. The food consumption at a nondrinking party always tips disproportionately in favour of sweets. A dry party is great fun for guests who are recovering alcoholics, since they don't have to be ever-watchful of alcohol lurking in the food. The people who refuse to attend a dry party can always be invited to another event for their turn at their own special fun. Both will love you, either way.

Business Entertaining

Entertaining for business is an important and indispensable part of getting to know clients and customers. It often provides the best possible background against which to discuss delicate points of negotiation, to thank a person or group for outstanding performance, to honour a member of the group, or to make a presentation of new products or ideas, to mention just a few of the reasons why business and entertaining are conducted simultaneously. Depending on the objective of the event or events, business entertaining may take place at any time of the day or evening. It can encompass all of the meals and events that tend to be the focus of your private entertainment events, with the notable exception of the major family holidays.

Business events are nearly always drinking events. Depending on the time of day, the nature of the event, the particular corporate culture, and the individuals involved, events can become virtual drinking marathons unless arrangements are made to allow each participant to find his or her own level of comfort where drinking is concerned. This means considering the wishes of the never-drinker, the recovering alcoholic, and the light, medium, and heavy social drinker as well as those of the dependent, drinking alcoholic. In my experience, it is the nondrinker who gets the least attention at business events. I have seen feverish attention paid to ensuring an adequate supply of the brands of wine and spirits favoured by a certain hard-drinking executive while the needs of his nondrinking colleagues were being largely ignored.

New directions for combining business with pleasure

In the last few years, the general attitude of participants at business events has undergone a marked change. The events themselves, however, lag far behind. It is not at all unusual, when seated at a dinner, to find that the only glasses provided are for wine. Of course, the waiter will go off and get you whatever you ask for, but this means that you have to wait, often with an open bottle of wine on the table tempting you to go ahead and have some anyway. It seems to me, and to many of the executives I spoke to during the writing of this book, that business events would be both more enjoyable and more productive if they were orientated toward encouraging less rather than more drinking.

I recently attended a large and festive business gathering that accomplished just this. It was a big, outdoor party for 500 of the host's employees, vendors, distributors, customers, and friends. Great attention had been paid to the food, which had been planned to provide a distinct regional flavour, in this case Midwestern, and all of it was home-made. Wine, beer, numerous varieties of soft drinks, and alcohol were all available, but not from the same location. The wine and beer were served from a single wagon. The soft drinks were all the way on the other side of the tent, all together, in giant tubs of ice. And in order to get to the alcohol, you had to walk the length of the tent, cross the car park, go into the office building, and find your way to the bar in one of the executive's offices. This is what I mean by orientating the event away from drinking. It isn't that you can't get what you want, it's that the non-alcoholic beverages are very easy to find, and you don't have to resist the alcohol to get to the soft stuff as you do when it's all on one bar. Since many people drove to this event, tilting it towards soft drinks was practical as well as considerate of the nondrinkers. The food helped too. It was wonderful. To ensure its authenticity, various special sources had been sought out and asked to produce their best dishes. There was a lot of this great food, and it was made available for the length of the party. After the food service was over, local entertainment was provided, and the coffee kept flowing. By that time most of us had forgotten all about the existence of an alcoholic bar. As we weren't smashed, we kept going for hours, and many valuable business discussions were held and many new acquaintances made during the evening. The affair was a resounding success.

Playing the power game

A 'power' event, in this context, has essentially come to mean one at which alcoholic beverages, if served at all, are spurned by the players of the power game, particularly by the most powerful players. Accompanying this concept of not drinking as a display of personal power is the concept of slightly eccentric timing. For example, why have a business breakfast at the ordinary hour of 8 a.m. or 8.30 a.m. when you can begin at 7 a.m. and have that much more time to talk? Drinking at that hour is out of the question from a social point of view and being able to rise and shine—and conduct business—at that hour says, without words, that you are on the ball, fit, and that you did not get smashed the night before. (Lest you think that this is true of all 7 a.m. breakfasters, see the section to follow on special techniques applicable to sales conferences and other overnight events.) If you really don't want to drink in the morning or have to watch someone else do it, the earlier the better for the business breakfast. The closer you get to the brunching hour, the more likely you are to have to deal with a request for a drink.

The term Power Lunch describes an event at which the key players not only seem to see who can drink the least, but to see who can eat the lightest meal. All of the finest expense-account restaurants have got the message, and offer delightful salads and other light dishes served in tiny portions. Superb wines are served by the glass in the better places, and are available in several choices—a long step from 'house' white or red. This development is a boon for those of us who want to take our drinking clients and colleagues to lunch but may not want to drink ourselves. We can happily order our nonalcoholic beverages while our guests can have a different wine with each course if that is what is wanted. Many of the restaurants known as wine bars offer an enormous array of wine by the glass to accompany elegant menus of light dishes such as patés, and salads. These kinds of restaurants have proliferated in metropolitan areas. If they haven't yet appeared in your area, why not suggest this style of business entertaining to the person who runs your favourite restaurant? The idea has merit for both of you. There is far more profit in selling a bottle of wine by the glass, and you will visit that restaurant far more often if it makes you truly comfortable.

Meanwhile, back at the power lunch, where you are naturally a key player (you're reading this book, aren't you?). You will, because of the setting, have no problem ordering your nonalcoholic whatever and something light to eat. A perfect way to begin the afternoon, since you won't be bothering with the cocktail hour (that's when you go to the gym to work out—right?), which means that you'll be really hungry by 4 p.m. and ready for the Power Tea.

The idea of tea as a business event is new enough to

give you the advantage of the element of surprise if you suggest it. One-up for you at the start is always nice. It is especially nice if you don't want to drink, as a tea is by definition a nondrinking event. Having eaten three lettuce leaves, one shrimp, one scallop, and two carrot straws for lunch, you will be starving by now; so will your guest, if he or she was also present at the nearly nonexistent power lunch. Starving people make for grouchy business discussions, so plan to provide something other than sweets to eat. If you are serving in the office and lack the facilities for anything fancy, you can cut a few light sandwiches into quarters, trim off the crusts, and voilà!—tea sandwiches. Cakes and biscuits can follow the sandwiches if you wish, and most of us do. Conversation over tea (or coffee, if that is the preferred beverage or, for that matter, a cold drink), and a light snack can be very productive. As with all other nonalcoholic events, because the participants are not getting tipsy they can continue the conversation at whatever level of intensity is required for a much longer period of time than they could if they were drinking.

We'll skip the cocktail hour (an increasingly common decision) and move smartly to the next event.

When a nonfood event can be the answer

Another alternative for business entertaining, and one that can be very effective, is to arrange for the main event to be a nonfood event. This might mean a concert, a trip to the theatre or the ballet, or a sports event. The choice depends on your guests' interests and your and their business objectives. If you don't drink and they do, focusing on a non-food event moves the emphasis away from drinking, directing it instead to the event and the business at hand.

Once, very early in my travelling days, I was competing with other publishing executives for the attention of a particular editor in the United Kingdom. At the time, I was having some wretched stomach problems in the aftermath of a bout with dysentery. As a result, I focused my entertaining on nonfood events whenever I could. In this case I was able to obtain tickets for The Horse of The Year Show at Wembley Stadium on a night when a member of the royal family would be on hand to present awards. I invited the editor to join me for the event and got an immediate acceptance. (Much later, I found out that he had turned down several dinner invitations in order to join me at the Horse Show.) Since the event did not require our absolute attention, it gave us ample time to talk business. This is a useful example of the advantage to be gained by thinking in terms of the element of surprise. Sometimes, in your quest to avoid major drinking, you can come up with treats that fit special needs and wishes of your guest (treats can be doubly pleasurable when they're unexpected), allow you to do whatever business you want, and also provide fresh, imaginative entertainment.

Another event that allows ample time for business discussion as well as easy accommodation for both drinkers and nondrinkers is the golf tournament. It's a nonfood event because in order to observe the action, you must follow the competitors around the course. Most people do not carry food with them on these rounds, and some courses have rules about where you can and can't carry food and drink. There is nearly always a dining room or coffee shop at the club or hotel where the tournament is being held, which means that the meal service is likely to be informal. Under these circumstances, you and your guests can drink or not drink, depending on your personal preferences, and you have little need to worry about alcohol turning up unexpectedly in the food.

Theatre, concerts, ballet and the like are events where your undivided attention is required during the performance. These are excellent events for occasions when lengthy discussions are not needed—when what you want is a general feeling of camaraderie. The only opportunity for drinking occurs during intermission, when the crowd at the bar is often so deep that it is easy to forgo the mid-performance drink. Soft drinks are frequently available at another, less crowded counter, as are snacks. Late supper is lighter than dinner and more naturally a nonalcoholic event than dinner.

We have noticed that only very few restaurants carry nonalcoholic beer, and nonalcoholic wine. This is really too bad, for many business people who are not recovering alcoholics often wish to avoid drinking beverages with the usual alcoholic content, perhaps because they are driving to or from the event. The tiny amounts of alcohol in nonalcoholic beer and wine are no problem to most people and it is our hope that these beverages will in the future be more readily available at restaurants.

Hitting the road without hitting the booze

Before we discuss overnight events such as sales conferences, I'd like to take a moment to discuss travelling without drinking. Under certain circumstances, this is more easily said than done. I know of at least one recovering alcoholic who slipped up during a first-class flight to an important meeting. It was his first taste of deluxe air travel and a reward for a job well done; however, no one thought about the dangers of his exposure to the bountiful quantities of free booze, not only in the drinks but in the food. Needless to say, the immediate results were unpleasant for all concerned. Happily, this executive is back on track; he now, however, flies in the back of the plane by choice.

We all know that drinking and driving don't mix, but less attention has been given to the debilitating effects of drinking alcohol during air travel. The alcohol increases dehydration, and, as many of us have discovered, small amounts can leave you not only with a 'cotton mouth' but also with a whopping headache and the urge to down copious quantities of water upon arrival. The best and most detailed discussions I have seen on the effects of combining alcohol with flying have appeared in various business magazines and newspapers and are primarily addressed to those who must learn to minimize the effects of flying across time zones. Buried in the articles, along with the other advice, is invariably the suggestion that you avoid drinking alcohol. It is ironic that as those of us who have chosen to work for large corporations work our way up the famed corporate ladder, we earn the right to more luxurious accommodations—the right to move out of the aircraft's tourist section to its business-class section and, ultimately, to first class, at least for long trips. In the course of this progress, we are presented with more and more opportunities to indulge in free booze. Most of us have had at least one experience, usually shortly after our 'elevations,' when we went a little too far with the freebies. This can be a valuable lesson in learning to summon the necessary discipline to say no to the drinks. I have spent the last 14 years doing a great deal of travelling, both in the U.S. and abroad, and there are still times when I have to work at avoiding the drink on the plane. The party atmosphere the airlines strive to create in business and first-class travel centres around alcohol. About the only nonalcoholic drink offered before takeoff is orange juice. If you can't drink that, you have to wait until after takeoff to get anything else. In tourist class you don't have this problem, but there will be times when, for legitimate business reasons, you really can't fly that way.

Over the years, I have devised a personal strategy for avoiding the alcohol on planes. First, I never board a plane when I am very hungry. Secondly, I try to schedule the flight for a time of day that is not a traditional drinking time. I avoid the dinner-hour flights because I can expect to have a hard time avoiding the drink and know that I will pay for any indulgence with a headache. Thirdly I always have a snack with me. Usually something sweet, like biscuits. I have no interest in an alcoholic drink with a sweet snack but will go out of my way to get a cup of tea to have with it. Fourthly I relax all of my other diet rules for the duration of the flight, which means that I can have the dessert and the bread if they look tempting. This makes avoiding the alcohol that much easier.

It annoys me, incidentally, when I fly in business or first class, avoiding drinks because I need to pop off that aircraft fresh as a daisy and go right into a meeting, that I have to pay the same airfare as the heavy boozers around me. At least in tourist class, if they drink, they pay.

Enough said about travel. Most of us fly because it is the most practical way to get from point A to point B quickly enough to accomplish our business. For short hauls, we sometimes drive or in certain locations can take a fast train. Driving allows us to remain in complete control, and trains are not the drinking trigger for me that they have been for friends with a history of being big buffet-car patrons on local commuter lines.

The bottom line on business travel is this: for top performance at your destination, don't drink alcohol en route.

Now let's discuss the destination itself.

The conference: decisions, decisions

For many of us, this destination is a sales conference or other company-sponsored meeting held at an airport or resort hotel. The group will work together, with only planned breaks, for anywhere from 3 to 7 days. The participants are at the mercy of the conference planner, who decides what they will eat and drink and when it will appear. The larger the group, the lower the flexibility in these matters. This kind of gathering is, for many of us, our first exposure to certain aspects of business entertaining. We are understandably a little edgy this first time out and, before we know it, can find ourselves in the midst of one booze-ridden event after another. If there is a hospitality suite, it is likely to be both the centre of activity and a prime source of excess alcohol. You need to be there to communicate with the conference participants, and you may spend hours in the place. There's usually a do-it-yourself bar with an ordinary assortment of beer, spirits, white wine, and soft drinks. The soda water always goes first as sharp nondrinkers keep their glasses filled with it—while it lasts. Some have been known to set aside a bottle or two early in the evening so that it will be available at midnight, when it's really needed. Food, if any, is invariably tired-looking, crisps, nuts, and pretzels—all saturated with salt and guaranteed to make you thirsty. It's next to impossible to resist nibbling on these mediocre offerings, especially when you will be working in this room for hours and you're already avoiding the alcoholic beverages. Because it is highly unlikely that the next hospitality suite you visit will have been redone to accommodate nondrinkers, we suggest that you have a substantial snack before entering it. Not enough to ruin your dinner, just enough to keep you from being interested in food and drink for two or three hours, during which there is bound to be a planned break. My favourite choice for this mini-meal is a bowl of soup served with biscuits, either sent up to the room or enjoyed in the coffee shop. Not clear consommé—something you can get your teeth into, like minestrone or tomato.

You will be better able to keep up with the marathon schedule of a business conference if you avoid alcoholic beverages. Those who must avoid them are apt to find the evening stint in the hospitality suite or the cocktail lounge the most difficult hurdle.

At most away-from-home conferences, activity begins early in the morning. Breakfast is usually substantial, and you would be well-advised to eat it. You may not get anything else until 1 p.m. or even later. There will be some kind of mid-morning break, at which food and drink may or may not feature. If they are supplied at all, both are reliably nonalcoholic. Lunch can be either a sit-down affair or a buffet served near the meeting rooms. Again, it is easy to avoid drinking. Food with alcohol in it is apt to be slightly more problematic at lunch, but is easily circumvented at a buffet and only rarely a problem at a sit-down event. If there is a sauce on the main dish and you can't have an alcohol-based sauce, you will want to converse with a waiter and may need to ask for an unsauced serving or for a substitution. If this happens, be prepared to wait for your plate to be delivered and be sure to urge the others at your table to start on their food, assuring them that you will catch up. You're the leader in this situation as the others will try to be polite, and at a big business gathering, there are several possible interpretations of 'polite.' In all my years of business lunches at conferences, I have only once been in a situation where no nonalcoholic beverage was available. Availability of nonalcoholic drinks is guaranteed at lunchtime.

Additional meetings may be scheduled for part or all of the afternoon, but there is bound to be at least a short break at the end of the afternoon to allow the participants to change for dinner. (There may or may not be food or drink available during a mid-afternoon break, but if anything is served, again, it is reliably nonalcoholic. Beer may be added to the beverages on hand at this time of day, but more often it is not.) Once the meetings break up for the pre-dinner intermission, you have your chance to prepare for the evening's activities. At a conference, they will last at least until midnight and quite possibly later. This type of event provides excellent opportunities to talk to colleagues about matters that you would probably not discuss otherwise. A major advantage of bringing everyone together away from the office is that it gives them a golden opportunity to renew, strengthen, and widen their contacts. Therefore, your preparations should be based on the assumption that it will be a long evening.

If the plan calls for two hours of drinking, followed by a dinner, followed by the de rigueur session in the hospitality suite, we recommend that you fortify yourself with food before you head for the cocktail hour. Here is where the soup comes in, or whatever else you fancy. If time is short, have it delivered to your room and snack while you get dressed. It doesn't matter how you manage it as long as you eat enough to hold you until dinner. (This interval also includes the amount of time between sitting down for dinner and actually getting something to eat.) We are now beginning the tricky time of day for nondrinking participants. For a recovering alcoholic, getting through this kind of evening can be like finding the right path through a maze. There's a possible problem at every turn. To begin with, there may be alcohol in some of the hors d'oeuvres. Wine in the cheese, brandy in the paté, and so on. This means either cautious tasting or abstaining. It is always possible to avoid the alcoholic drinks, but they don't always make it easy for you. The soft drinks are likely to be on the bar with the hard drinks. You may have to reach past the hard ones to get the soft ones you want. They may run out of the soft drinks and have to send for more. Someone may try to push a nonalcoholic drink on you at an awkward moment. It can be difficult to explain the ramifications of .05 percent alcohol, especially when the container may not be marked. If you're not hungry, you'll have a much easier time of all this. It won't matter what is being served, and you won't have to brave the wet bar more than once since you won't be all that thirsty.

The next hurdle is the dinner itself. Tables are often set with wine glasses only. You have to ask for water. You might as well start right away. If you can get a waiter to deliver the water before food service starts, you won't have to wait until the first course is served to get your drink. Alternatively, you may be able to peek at the set-up tables from the cocktail area to see whether there are provisions for water and, if there aren't, to fill up at the bar before going in to be seated.

As it has become increasingly fashionable to pass up red meat in favour of poultry and fish, conference dinners have become more difficult for recovering alcoholics. The probability of encountering a white wine sauce rises sharply when poultry or fish are served. As gourmet cooking has assumed the status of a national hobby, hotels and restaurants have been inspired to create more elaborate sauces, and in haute cuisine this means a wine-based sauce. Gone are the days of the simple slab of roast beef served au jus. Recovering alcoholics will have to decide whether or not they are willing to chance the wine-based sauces and act accordingly. Because of mass preparation techniques, the chances of any real alcohol being left in the sauce are slim, but they will bear the winey taste of their origins. It is up to you. If you decide against it, ask for the dish without the sauce or for a substitution. I once sat by a guest who refused the duck à l'orange. The duck couldn't be served without the sauce as all of the servings of duck had already been sauced. Instead, my neighbour got the most beautiful slice of roast beef, sauced au jus, and happily carved away. As always, be prepared to wait a few minutes for your request to be filled. Make a special effort to keep others at your table at their ease, and eating, while you wait.

Dessert may or may not be for you. Taste carefully or have a neighbour taste; gourmet treats may drip with spirits.

If after-dinner drinks are served while you are still at

table, have your second cup of coffee or tea while the others get to work on their headaches.

We now return to the hospitality suite, which is where we started this conference and where we leave you. If you have any influence on such matters, perhaps you can get someone to deliver finger sandwiches at midnight.

A small and final word about attending business events. You will from time to time run into a needy, drinking alcoholic. In the name of successful entertaining, never deny this person a drink. To drink or not is an individual decision and while I am obviously advocating directing business entertainment away from alcohol, I do not believe that forcing dry events on business people is wise. Above all, the event, whatever it is, should go smoothly so that your primary attention may be given to business. Planning primarily nonalcoholic events merely makes it easier for some of your guests or participants to function.

Planning the Business Gathering

Nowhere do party planners face greater potential for problems than at a business gathering. To begin with, you don't know your guests as well as you do your personal friends, so you're not likely to know who isn't drinking out of choice and who can't drink. Therefore, such gatherings are approached as mixed events, drinkers and nondrinkers, and the fixed menu should involve no alcohol unless the item is cooked for such a long time that there is no possibility of the spirits remaining, though even that should be avoided if possible. Raw alcohol, such as is found in fruit cups, salad dressings, and desserts should not be introduced.

Breakfast or Tea Instead of Cocktails?

If you are hosting and it's just a meeting with one or two

others, you can focus on a nondrinking occasion like an early breakfast or afternoon tea. At breakfast, chances are no one will ask for a drink, and if someone wants one at tea, that's easy.

I have never been in a situation at a larger event where I couldn't get a nonalcoholic drink, but if this should happen to you, just ask for what you want. It will almost certainly be the result of an oversight. Most people are sufficiently sensitive to the existence of nondrinkers and alternative beverages are usually supplied, especially when the affairs are professionally arranged.

Major Events

If you work for a corporation and are in charge of major business events, this is your chance to try some of our suggestions. We think it most effective to meet with the hotel and/or caterer at least a week in advance to explain what you want to do. The concept of wet and dry bars in different locations may be new to their food and beverage professionals. Depending on their clientele, they may also have to work outside their standard menu range to come up with an imaginative menu that will appeal to your group without relying on the usual wine sauces and soused deserts. Given a little time, they can collaborate with you to produce the kind of mixed affair you want.

Lunch, Dinner, and Conference Suggestions

The short, nonalcoholic power lunch, whether large or small, often allows only 15 or 20 minutes for the total group to arrive before lunch is served. Most people seem to arrive in the last 10 minutes and ignore the bar, which these days is usually a cash–and–carry affair.

Dinner for business is usually in a restaurant, and in my view should not exceed 10 people unless you get a large round table for 12. Otherwise you must divide the group—with some accounting for status—into two tables of six or more. These dinners are also held late more often than not in order to allow leisurely time for conducting business. Yes, this means that the guests may be hungry to the point of irritation. If they do drink in the absence of nourishment, they will feel the effects immediately. For this type of business dinner, I recommend pre-ordering a light appetizer and two beverages, one alcoholic and one not, to be served immediately after seating while the guests are deliberating over the menu. Tell the maitre d'hôtel that you would appreciate (emphasis on the word) glasses in two different shapes. Small savoury toasts are ideal for menu-browsing as they are easy to handle while perusing the card. This little bit of food will erase your irritation problem and get the party off to a better start.

If you are planning a sales conference, management seminar, or other overnight event, you can reduce the consumption of alcohol in the hospitality suite by providing attractive snacks for people to sample. Late-night people will welcome pastry and coffee and can probably be counted on to pass up the last nightcap for the sweets. I once saw a room full of two-fisted drinkers abandon their booze for coffee and three trays of miniature French pastries, as quick as lightning, the beasts! Just be sure to include decaffeinated beverages in any late-night snacks or you may have some late-night-prowlers, sober but prowling in search of sleep.

If possible, skip the cocktail party. If you want a late-afternoon event, serve tea. The drinks will be coming up at dinner.

Late supper is a nice idea if it fits into your schedule. You can effectively use lunch or brunch menus for supper. Just remember the decaffeinated beverages.

Whatever you decide, plan your event to smooth the way for the business at hand. The food and drink are background, and the desired result of your careful planning is for everyone to be completely comfortable and unaware of the extent of your efforts.

Restaurant Dining

Eating out is one of the great pleasures of life, at least to me. I never realized that to a recovering alcoholic it's more like setting out to cross a mine field until I was asked to serve as a taster by a couple of friends who must avoid any alcohol in their food and who, in addition, do not care for the taste of wine or other alcohol-containing sauces even if all the alcohol has been cooked out. This was a revelation to me. One told me that she does not go to French restaurants without a friend to taste the food as she has found that the management and waiters don't understand that a little bit can hurt. Once you have explained matters to the staff, my experience is that most restaurant personnel will bend themselves backwards to be sure that you don't get any alcohol by mistake. The trick: get them to really understand. Here's one technique used by a friend:

Waiter: Can I get you something to drink?

Friend: Yes, I'd like a plain tonic with a slice of lime and would you please bring the menu right away.
Waiter scurries off to get drink and menu.

Friend looks over menu. Safe dishes include most roasted and grilled meat except for steak Diane or any other dish that is either flamed or has alcohol in the finishing sauce. Dishes with sauces cooked for a long time will have had the alcohol cooked out of the sauce, but the residual taste stays on. I find that recovered alcoholics vary as to whether or not they are willing to eat these dishes, so in a restaurant it is merely a matter of choice.

Waiter: Have you decided?
Friend: Yes, I see three dishes that look good, but I'd
              like to ask you about how they are prepared
              before deciding.

*A conversation with the waiter about exactly how
the dishes are prepared then follows. The waiter
may go to the kitchen to ask the chef. If he returns
to report that only a 'little bit' of alcohol exists in a
dish, explain that you are allergic and must not
have any at all—just like someone allergic to
shellfish, let us say, or to pork. The food arrives
and so does the moment of truth. One taste will tell
the tale: either the restaurant wants you back or it
doesn't. There is no need to give up wonderful food
just because you don't want to eat the alcohol you
no longer drink.*

Menu Mysteries—how to solve them

Most restaurants' chefs don't realize what havoc the
alcohol in food can cause and see no reason for publishing
ingredients ahead of your asking about the contents of
the dishes.

Alcohol can be found in nearly any part of the meal,
not just in the beverage, which one sips with caution
anyway. It can emerge in any dish that is devilled.
Flaming dishes require alcohol to fuel the flame and are to
be completely avoided because the alcohol is never completely dissipated by the flaming. Unfortunately, alcohol
can also lie in wait in ordinary dishes, salad dressings, and
desserts.

Asking for Alternatives

Always ask about the dishes that interest you. Then, if
you frequent the restaurant, you'll become completely

familiar with the menu. You are purchasing the food, it is yours, and so is your body.

I like to investigate new restaurants with friends and come back later with clients or other guests. If a restaurant can properly handle a party in which some member must avoid alcohol, then it will look after everyone else properly as well.

Sometimes a restaurant will alter a menu for your guest if you like everything about it except the poverty of nonalcoholic choices. We frequently return to one which did just this by adding at least one nonalcoholic dessert to the menu and by being unfailingly willing to prepare another, without alcohol, on request.

Don't start thinking that asking for nonalcoholic food will cause a big fuss and attract unwanted attention to you. If the restaurant is good, and if your host/hostess knows in advance that you don't eat foods that contain alcohol, your requests become part of the usual conversation that would precede ordering in any good restaurant. If it becomes apparent that the waiter will be commuting to and from the kitchen with your questions, you have a couple of choices. You can ask all your questions at once and give the waiter alternatives, or you can ask the waiter to come back with the answers so you can choose. I prefer the latter because many chefs will offer wonderful alternatives to the listed sauce, ones which may prove more delightful than what is on the menu.

When you are host/hostess at dinner in your favourite restaurant, you control the ordering, and presumably you and the restaurant know one another so you can feel at home and comfortable about offering menu suggestions to anyone in your party who doesn't drink.

Breakfast Out

Breakfasts, like tea, do not attract hard-core drinkers unless they have been up all night drinking and are not ready for reality without more alcohol at an early break-fast. Typically, any gathering before 10 a.m. is a time for sobriety, a no-drinking occasion. If a person is a 'needy' drinker, he or she will 'fortify' themselves before arriving to have breakfast with you. (Quotes are sympathetically intended.)

If breakfast is at home, check the Brunch section for menu ideas and order of service.

If it is to be out, find a local restaurant or hotel whose food and service are to your liking.

CHAPTER SIX

Special Occasions—Ideas and Menus

We all enjoy special occasions, and the year isn't full enough of them if we only observe the public holidays. Add to those weddings, confirmations, bar mitzvahs, engagement parties, birthdays, anniversaries, and so on, and you have many opportunities to join friends for a good time.

Since a special occasion is 'special' and an 'occasion' it usually means a more elaborate menu and almost certainly a mixed group of drinkers and nondrinkers, with the drinkers expecting to live it up a bit. Of course, the nondrinkers may out-live 'em and out-last 'em, but that is an ineffable secret known best to nondrinkers.

Sentimental occasions in particular seem to inspire people to imbibe and, as most of us know, nothing is more charged than a family celebration soused with alcohol.

The first year I had a group New Year's Eve with a few recovering alcoholics among the guests, I provided some very nice wine and sparkling apple juice for everyone. We quickly ran out of the juice and I found to my surprise that we had wine left over. Given the choice, the drinkers were busy drinking the nondrinkers' drink. That experience aroused my curiosity and I began experimenting with menu, order of service, beverages, etc., so that my parties gradually became more nonalcoholic. I wanted to see what would happen. No one seemed to notice the change. If a guest looked for a drink, I gave it readily, with apology. If not, they could choose from several goodies since the get-together was primarily non-drinking, and the nonalcoholic drinks enjoyed the spotlight more than the alcoholic drinks. With each succeeding year, my entertaining became successfully more nonalcoholic, while new food and drink continued to be introduced, tried, and welcomed.

As you'll note, the basic suggestions for nonalcoholic events apply to special occasions as well. A short cocktail hour with plenty of food and prompt service of the meal, easily distinguishable glasses for alcoholic beverages (if served at all), no booze in any of the food, and abundant quantities of food.

Here are some menus for special occasions:

New Year's Day— leftovers instead of hangovers

In place of hangovers, 'Leftovers' has become a tradition with us because we always have a glowing New Year's Eve party which rounds off a three-week period of reactionary rebellion against dieting (and health). We hold The Leftover at around 4 p.m. on New Year's Day for those who missed the big party and serve all of the leftovers in a brunch-like affair, at the end of which we pack up leftover-leftovers for our stuffed guests and dispatch them home. It marks the end of the holiday season at our house; the end of a good year, the start of a better one. As with all Leftover parties, it is a matter of mechanical assembly of remainders. We serve buffet style and do it plain. Here is what we might have:

Fresh raw vegetables and low-fat onion dip
Cold sliced meat loaf,★ turkey, and ham
Cold turkey stuffing, cranberry sauce

★ Recipe included

Hot bacon, noodle, tomato, and cheese casserole★
Large tossed salad with a light vinaigrette dressing
Cakes, biscuits, sweets, and all manner of goodies
Beverages: leftover Christmas punch, sparkling apple juice, hot or cold mulled apple juice,★ water. Coffee and tea with the sweet things.

If you enjoy carefree entertaining, this has got to be one of your favourite parties. There is very little work involved in setting out the food, you don't have to get dressed up, you can review the previous night's party with choice friends, and you end up with practically no leftovers from the Leftover. A Happy New Year to all!

Shrove Tuesday—or 'Pancake Day' as it has come to be known

Although not celebrated as much in this country as in others where it is the final climactic day of the Carnival, we do have our own tradition of eating pancakes with sugar and lemon. If you are partial to rich sweet things why not serve them with our non-alcoholic hard sauce★, preferably hot so the sauce will melt into creamy pools of rich delicious goo.

The following is a suggested menu for the last day before Lent . . .

Tossed green salad with green peppers and cherry tomatoes; vinaigrette dressing

Roast veal au jus

Steamed green beans

Puréed carrots★

Pancakes (Crêpes)★ with hard sauce★

★ Recipe included

In view of the light meal, the dessert itself should be kept relatively rich.

St. Paddy's Day—
the eatin' of the green

Faith and begorrah, except for New Year's Eve and maybe your 40th birthday, there are few holidays that encourage the 'curse of the Irish' more than wonderful and grand ol' St. Paddy's day. I went to college in a town that allowed only 'near' beer (3 percent alcohol) to be served to students. Every St. Patrick's Day, the local pubs coloured this stuff with green food colouring and the student body drank itself silly. People would be lurching around like leprechauns with green lips and tongues until they could hold no more, often turning green in the face as well.

It may be sacrilegious and an insult to St. Paddy to have a nonalcoholic party where you don't serve a drop of 'how-do-you-do,' but where there is plenty of cheery St. Patrick's green on the table may the good saint forgive me if I say that my choice for this party is either a tea in the afternoon—I said it, and I'm glad—or a dessert party in the evening, audacious as it may seem on this auspicious occasion when alcohol marches to the skirl of bagpipes.

The menu below is for a tea party, but could easily be adjusted for supper.

Green cream-cheese sandwiches (white bread with green colour cream cheese, or if your local bakery makes green bread, use it with white cheese—be sure to cut off the crusts as the green food colouring doesn't look too appetizing in the crust. If you use white bread, to trim or not to trim is up to you)

Stuffed celery (with low-fat blue cheese or cheddar spread)

Cherry tomatoes, lettuce garnish

Sliced boiled ham, turkey, and cheese sandwiches, combined as you like

Cottage cheese salad on a bed of greens

Chocolate and yellow cupcakes or squares with green icing

Green and white pinwheel biscuits

Green and white sugar mints

Beverages: coffee, tea, sparkling apple juice, fizzy water

Easter—traditional elegance

There are many traditional dishes for Easter dinner, most of which do not require booze in the food, so this holiday gives you a number of choices as you are not up against a predominantly drinking occasion. Nevertheless, alcohol will find its way into some things, so here is a menu that will avoid alcohol for sure.

Chicory with sour cream and salmon caviar

Glazed baked ham with cloves

Raisin sauce

Spring asparagus, steamed

Baked sweet potatoes

Coconut cake with raspberry filling

Beverage: sparkling apple juice, sparkling water, non-alcoholic sparkling wine

Whitsun Bank Holiday—a parade of old-fashioned dishes

Now known, somewhat unappealingly, as 'Spring' Bank Holiday, this isn't celebrated as much as it once was which is a pity—especially as it comes at such a nice time of the year. When I was a child, we always came home after church and had a family party in the garden if weather permitted. Some years we had the usual hot dogs and hamburgers; others, we had special baked, marinated pork chops (which I still like).

So for old time's sake here is an updated Whitsunday menu:

Salted and unsalted pretzels

Devilled cheese on biscuits, served hot

Baked, marinated pork chops

Homemade baked beans

Tossed green salad

Chocolate biscuit refrigerator cake

Beverages: nonalcoholic beer, sparkling apple juice, sparkling water

That Day at the Races, School Sports Day or Summer Fête

We all have those summer occasions when we like to (or have to) dress up and produce a superior picnic. Here is a menu which works well and is always popular:

Herbed brie with biscuits

Cold sliced roast beef, turkey breast, and gruyère cheese

Homemade potato salad

Tossed green garden salad, with several kinds of lettuce, sliced radishes, diced sweet green and red pepper, fresh garden peas (or use frozen, thawed but not cooked), mushrooms, spring onions, celery, parsley, fresh herbs tossed with a light lemon vinaigrette dressing

Old fashioned strawberry shortcake, whipped cream

Beverages: mineral water, soft drinks, iced tea, non-alcoholic beer

August Bank Holiday—end-of-summer favourites

With its hint of autumnal nostalgia in the air, this Bank Holiday is always a wonderful time to have a party with all of the special end-of-summer fruits and vegetables in season. There is so much to choose from, it's hard to decide, but this menu combines some of my all-time favourites.

Sliced tomatoes, purple onion, green pepper, tuna, and parsley salad

Grilled poussins (baby chickens)

Corn on the cob

Fresh green beans with slivered almonds

Vanilla ice cream with fresh peaches, melba and zabaglione* sauces

* Receipe included

Halloween—treats with no tricks

This is always a time for fun. The harvest is in, turnip-lanterns are lit, the weather is just beginning to chill, and the autumn social season is upon us. My favourite party for Halloween is a post trick-or-treat★ party to be held around 8 p.m. or so in the evening. It's not meant to last too long, as the next day is usually a weekday and people need to be able to get home before too late to avoid the little hobgoblins out to get 'em on this haunted night.

Fresh apple juice, cold or hot and mulled or Old English Norfolk Punch

Fresh, hot doughnuts (shop bought, and heated in the oven at 150°C/300°F/Gas Mark 2 for 10 minutes, which will work for anything except iced and glazed doughnuts)

Mouse-trap cheddar cheese

Biscuits

Sliced apples

Platter of parboiled vegetables, served cold with an onion dipping sauce. These can include green beans, broccoli, cauliflower, turnips, and carrots.

Beverages: coffee and tea in addition to apple juice for those who don't want a sweet drink

---

★ An American tradition just beginning to catch-on in this country is to send the children 'trick-or-treating'. This means they go around the neighbours, knocking on doors and asking for a 'treat'. The neighbours are supposed to have a supply of sweets to appease the children and if they don't the children will play a trick on them.

Christmas Eve— dreaming of a White Christmas Supper

In some countries, the theme for this gentle dinner is traditionally all-white. I can never resist the touch of colour, though, so here is my version of the menu:

Chicory salad, vinaigrette dressing

Poached fillets of sole, no-wine cream sauce with mushrooms★

Rice pilaf

Steamed mange-trout peas

A light sponge cake with white fondant icing★, decorated with Christmas angels

Beverages: nonalcoholic champagne, sparkling cider, coffee and tea with dessert.

Christmas Day—all of the trimmings, but none of the usual hard stuff

At our house this is traditionally a roast with all the holiday trimmings. Regardless of the roast, the trimmings seem to be substantially the same.

Nonalcoholic eggnog★

Celery and carrot sticks

Hot sliced German-style sausage

Salami and cream cheese wheels

Roast turkey, 2 stuffings, gravy

Roast potatoes

Mashed potatoes

★ Recipe included

Puréed carrots★

Brussel sprouts

Cranberry Sauce

Nonalcoholic plum pudding served hot with hard sauce★and foamy sauce★

Chocolate after-dinner mints

Beverages: sparkling water, sparkling apple juice, sparkling nonalcoholic burgundy (and sparkling guests!), coffee and tea with dessert

New Year's Eve—keeping both drinkers and nondrinkers happy

This is one of the biggest parties of the year for many people and it can be a difficult time for those who have chosen not to drink. With so much holiday cheer around, it is second nature to raise the glass and to have it filled with an alcoholic beverage.

There are many ways to celebrate New Year's Eve. What happened at my New Year's Eve parties over a period of nearly five years is in great part responsible for this book. As my guests' tastes changed, the party changed. The starting time is now earlier, the food is more abundant, and is served from the beginning of the party. The main punch bowl is 'dry' and there are wet and dry bars for the guests. It's a mixed party, with guests who drink and guests who don't and they attend in about equal numbers. Partly because it is a time of year for 80-proof cheer, I tilt the party toward indulging the nondrinkers. Everybody's happy. So is the New Year!

Here is the menu from last year's party, which began promptly at 9 p.m. and wrapped itself up around 3 a.m.

★ Recipe included.

Fresh vegetables, raw and parboiled, crisps, and onion dip

Green olives

Pitted black olives

Mixed nuts

Medium wheel of mature cheddar cheese with biscuits

Blue-vein brie, biscuits

Homemade meat loaf,★ served warm

Roast turkey

Baked, glazed ham with cloves

Homemade baked beans

Green salad

Fruitcake, both kinds, brandied and without

Brownies

Iced butterscotch date brownies★

Hazelnut Christmas biscuits

Chocolate Walnut fudge

Beverages: fruit punch, mineral waters, distilled alcohol, champagne (rosé), red and white wine, soft drinks, coffee, tea

The order of service is fixed by tradition; while the beverages have changed over the years, it has remained constant. Guests usually arrive promptly, so all the appetizers are out and ready to be enjoyed by 8.45 p.m. When the doorman buzzes to announce the first guests, we lower the lights and light the candles on the tables and on the chandelier and pour the first bowl of punch.

★ Recipe included

Around 10 p.m. the hors d'oeuvres are moved to the side and the main meal is introduced on the dining room table for the guest stampede. When all is ready we announce that dinner is served and leap out of the way. One year I forgot the bugle, all the guests kept waiting politely for me to start, and I was busy doing something else for ten minutes or so before I realized what was happening.

Desserts are put out around 11.15 p.m., when we open the champagne and sparkling apple juice. The pink champagne is served because its colour distinguishes it from the apple juice. Different-shaped glasses are used to further distinguish the drinks. From that moment until all the guests have left, the champagne and apple juice keep flowing.

Coffee and tea are available throughout the evening, but most people like it with dessert.

The punch bowl is kept filled until the champagne and apple juice are served, then I let it run dry unless someone prefers to stay with the punch, in which case it gets filled, half a bowl at a time. Both bars stay open for the entire evening.

Brandied or other spiked food items are placed near the wet bar.

At midnight many of the guests gather around the TV set to watch the scene in Trafalgar Square and after a midnight's toasting, we stay in London via television with the promising excitement of the New Year; the last guests leave around 3 a.m.

A super ending to a great year and some terrific holiday entertainments.

CHAPTER SEVEN

Menus

Breakfast

*Poached Pears**

Scrambled Eggs

Thin, Crisp Bacon

*Popovers**

Butter, Margarine, Jam, Honey

Coffee, Tea, Juice, Water

★ Recipe included

Brunch I

Cheese Tray,
Featuring Mild Cheeses such as
Caerphilly, Brie, Gouda, Edam, and Cream

Small Slices of Bread, Warmed, Bite-sized Pastries

Raw Vegetables, Celery, Carrots

Eggs Florentine with Ham

Toast, Croissants, Brioches, Jam, Honey

Sparkling Fruit Juices, Nonalcoholic Wine (white),
Orange Juice with soda and Strawberry Juice, Sparkling Water

Coffee, Tea

Brunch II

Fresh Fruit Cup

Chicken Vol-au-Vents (Volleyballs)★

Lettuce and Grilled Tomato Garnish

Sparkling Apple Juice, Fizzy Water,

Champagne, White Wine,

Coffee, Tea

★ Recipe included

Brunch III

Large Tray of Vegetable Sticks and Decorative Lettuce

Sliced Fruit, Bite Size, to be Picked up on Cocktail Sticks

French Toast, Syrup, Butter

Sausages

Meringues

Sparkling Water with Fruit Slices,
Mimosas
Coffee, Tea

Brunch IV: Seated

Individual Bowls of Fruit Salad

Asparagus and Cheese Crêpes★

Grilled Tomatoes, Lettuce Garnish

Croissants, Sweet Rolls, Butter, Jam, Honey

Champagne, Sparkling Water with Pineapple Juice,
Coffee, Tea

★ Recipe included

Lunch I

First survey all the listed brunch menus. These are easily translated for lunch by eliminating the fruit and juice and adding a green salad.

Mixed Nuts, Crisps

Mushroom Consommé with Cheese Straws

Cold Sliced Lobster, Curry Mayonnaise★, Chutney, Sliced Egg

Cold Green Beans, Dressed

Fruit Sorbet, Wafers

Champagne (pink) and Sparkling Apple Juice to Start; can Switch to a White or Rosé Wine (don't forget the nonalcoholic selection), Iced Tea, or Sparkling Water

★ Recipe included

Lunch II

Cheese Spread and Wholewheat Biscuits

Onion Hamburgers, Mushroom Sauce

Lettuce and Tomato Salad

Three-Flavour Parfait

Beer and Nonalcoholic Beer,
Red Wine, with or without Alcohol,
Still Apple Juice

Lunch III

Green Olives, Bombay Mix

Bacon, Noodle, Tomato and Cheese Casserole★

Three-Green Tossed Salad

French Bread

Profiteroles with Butterscotch Sauce

Beer and Nonalcoholic Beer,
Red Wine, with or without Alcohol,
Still Apple Juice

★ Recipe included

Dinner I

Small Slices of Cheese, Biscuits

Smoked Salmon, Lemon, Onion, Capers, Buttered Whole Wheat Bread

Roast Veal, Gravy, Carrots, Onions, Green Beans

Watercress and Mushroom Salad

Apple Tart, Whipped Cream

*Apéritif Wine, Sparkling Apple Juice, Sparkling Water
White Wine with the entrée
(see alcohol-free wine section)*

Dinner II

Mixed Nuts, Mushroom Toasts★

Lady Curzon Soup★

Chicken Breasts in Cream★ Mange-tout·Peas, Sliced Courgettes

Lettuce and Tomato Salad

Chocolate Loaf Cake, Hard Sauce★

*Apéritif Wine, Sparkling Apple Juice, Sparkling Water
White Wine with the entrée
(see alcohol-free wine section)*

★ Recipe included

Dinner III

Stuffed Celery

Green Olives

Chicken Liver Paté,★ Melba Toast

Grilled Lamb Chops, Braised Chicory, Mashed Potatoes

Grilled Tomato Garnish

Mixed Salad

Coeur à la Crème, Strawberries

Apéritif Wine, Sparkling Apple Juice, Sparkling Water
White Wine with the entrée
(see alcohol-free wine section)

★ Recipe included

Late Night Supper I

First, check the lunch and brunch menus.
The main dishes, salads, and desserts from these menus
can easily be adjusted for late night supper, plus—

Relish Dish with Celery Sticks, Radishes, Carrot Straws

Stuffed Olives

Devilled Chicken Livers★

Rice Pilaf

Steamed Carrots

Pavlova with Kiwi and Cream★

Alcohol-Free Champagne,
Coffee, Tea, including decaffeinated versions,
Sparkling Water

★ Recipe included.

Late Night Supper II

Chinese Leaves and Chicory Salad

Poached Salmon with Bearnaise Sauce

Mange-Tout Peas, Boiled Potatoes

Hot Coffee-Chocolate★ with Whipped Cream and Petits Fours★

Sparkling Water with a Slice of Lemon or Lime
Nonalcoholic Wine, White or Rosé
Plain Coffee or Tea for anyone who doesn't drink chocolate

A Spring Supper

Hot Asparagus with Bacon or Ham served on a bed of Greens, Hollandaise Sauce

Herbed Fresh Tomatoes (preferably Cherry)

Petit Fours★

Iced Tea, Sparkling Water with a Slice of Lemon or Lime, Nonalcoholic White or Rosé Wine

★ Recipe included

CHAPTER EIGHT

Recipes

Warm Greetings: Soups and Stocks

Among the dishes that tend to hide an unbelievable amount of alcohol is the simple-looking soup. Here are some recipes that can be varied slightly, depending on how rich you want to make them, are very elegant, and yet contain no alcohol whatsoever.

Two elegant soups and a make-ahead party dish from one magical recipe

Carrot Soup

1 large leek, cleaned and chopped
— or —
1 medium onion, chopped
1 medium potato, peeled and cubed
1¼kg/2½lbs carrots (11 to 12 medium), peeled and
   sliced
1½ litres/2½ pints chicken stock
1½ tsps ground thyme
salt (optional; remember the chicken stock is salted)
½ tsp ground black pepper

Put everything in a pot, bring it to the boil, and simmer until tender. With a slotted spoon, transfer the solids to a blender or food processor and purée until smooth. I am deliberately a little sloppy about getting every last piece of solid into the food processor as I like the texture of a few unprocessed bits in the soup. Return the puréed mixture to the pot; thin if necessary with a little chicken stock to bring to the proper consistency. Return to heat and bring to the boil. This soup may be served hot or cold.

Serves four as a main course, six as an appetizer

Curried Carrot Soup

You can make a delightful curried version of this soup with the same recipe by omitting the thyme and adding 2 teaspoons of a medium-hot curry powder after the puréeing. (The curry is not part of the original cooking.) If you choose to flavour with curry, you must simmer the soup for about half an hour after you add the curry powder.

Puréed Carrots

The basic purée recipe for carrot soup may also be used for puréed carrots, which make an excellent side dish in place of mashed potatoes with any number of roast meats. For puréed carrots use only about 400 ml/¾ pint of chicken stock or the same amount of hot water with 2 bouillon cubes. Add 1¼kg/2½ pounds of carrots, 1 small yellow onion, and ½ to 1 teaspoon of thyme, depending on how strongly you want it flavoured. Simmer until tender, remove solids, purée in food processor or blender. If the texture is too thick, which is unlikely, add a little bit of the cooking liquid to bring it to the desired density. In this case I'm careful to purée every bit, as I don't think anyone wants lumps in their puréed carrots. This is handy party dish as it can be prepared a day in advance and then simply reheated.

Serves six

Cauliflower Soup

1 medium head of cauliflower, cut into florets
800 ml/1½ pints of chicken stock, fat removed
½ tsp ground black pepper
1½ tsps medium-hot curry powder (optional)
salt to taste (remember, there is salt in the chicken
   stock)

Trim the cauliflower, place in the chicken stock, bring to the boil and simmer until tender. With a slotted spoon, spoon most of the cauliflower into a blender or food processor, or put through a food mill until it is smooth. This soup is more attractive if you don't purée absolutely every little bit, so I usually leave a few of the smaller florets in the chicken stock to give the soup an interesting texture. Return the purée to the pot, add additional chicken stock or even plain water to bring it to the proper consistency. Depending on the amount of starch in the cauliflower, the soup may need to be thinned. If you desire a richer soup, this thinning can be done with double cream. Return the soup to the heat and bring to the simmer. Add the seasonings to taste, being careful with the curry, which begins to taste bitter if you use too much. This soup is equally good hot or cold. I usually serve it with finely chopped chives or spring onion tops as a garnish.

Serves four as a main course, six as an appetizer

This recipe came from a friend's mother and is one of the best I have ever tasted.

Cream of Tomato Soup

25g/1 oz butter
40 g/1½ oz flour
1½ tsps salt (optional)
⅛ tsp pepper
400 ml/¾ pint milk
450 g/ 1 lb tin of tomatoes
1 tbs minced onion
¼ tsp celery seed
½ tsp salt
100 g/4 oz sugar
½ bay leaf
1 whole clove
tiny pinch of bicarbonate of soda

Make white sauce and set aside. This is the base of many different sauces and is considered difficult by some. If you follow the instructions your sauce will never be lumpy; you'll always get the results you want.

White Sauce

Melt the butter over low heat in a saucepan. When the butter begins to bubble a little around the edges, add the flour all at once. If your flour has been sitting around for a while and is beginning to get a bit lumpy, sift the flour and then weigh it so you won't have to deal with lumps. Whisk the flour into the butter and continue to cook over low heat for about 2 minutes, just until you get a nice flour/butter paste. Remove the saucepan from the heat. Add the milk very slowly, beginning with just a dribble at a time. Your flour/butter mixture will be very thick and almost unmanageable at first. It will appear to lump but as long as you do not have the pan on the heat it will not. Continue to add the milk slowly; you'll watch it go through various stages of thickness, gradually thinning to a kind of soupy consistency. Then, as you add the last of the milk, it becomes no thicker than the milk itself. (You may use skimmed milk if you wish to reduce the calories in the recipe.) When the milk and the flour/butter mixture are well combined (there should be no remaining lumps or bits in corners of the pan), return the mixture to low to medium heat and stir constantly while you bring it to the boil. What you will have initially is . . . well . . . nothing; but then, as the mixture gets a bit warmer, just at the simmer point, you will notice—at last!—that it begins to thicken fairly quickly. This is a medium white sauce recipe, which will give you exactly the right texture for this particular soup. After the sauce has thickened, add the pepper and some of the salt if you wish, although I prefer to hold the salt until I've got the rest of the recipe together and can more accurately judge the final taste. Meanwhile, combine the tomato, onion, celery seed, sugar, bay leaf, and clove and cook until the onion is soft. This shouldn't take more than about 20 minutes. Remove from the heat, and if you have time, allow to cool for an hour or so, during which time the bay leaf and clove will lend additional flavour to the mixture. Remove the bay leaf and clove, process the tomato mixture until it's smooth in either a blender or a food processor, stir in the pinch of bicarb, and set aside.

To serve, combine the white sauce and the tomato mixture, stirring together, and heat but do not bring to the boil. Be very careful about this, as the soup will separate if you should inadvertently bring it to the boil. If this does happen, don't despair, as it won't destroy the taste; the texture can be restored by taking the whole mess and putting it back into the processor or blender and blending. It will not have quite the same smooth appearance as it would have otherwise, but the mixture will be just as palatable.

Serves 4

This elegant first course is said to have been invented by Lady Curzon during her stay in India as wife of the Viceroy. Although the original recipe calls for turtle soup, our version spares the turtle.

Lady Curzon Soup

800 ml/1½ pints rich beef stock or Campbell's consommé
1 tbs tomato paste
1 tbs onion, chopped
1 tbs celery, chopped
1 medium carrot, diced
1 tsp medium-hot curry powder
150 ml/¼ pint cream whipped, (the real thing—you can't substitute in this recipe)

Combine the stock, tomato paste, vegetables, and curry, and cook until the vegetables are very tender. Whip the cream until it is quite stiff and reserve in the refrigerator.

Just before serving, pour the hot soup into individual oven-proof cups or small ramekins, cover it generously with the whipped cream, and place the cups under a preheated grill for a minute or two to glaze the cream and brown it slightly.

Serves six

Two successful shortcut recipes that can be used in any recipe calling for beef stock: as a soup; or as a brown stock to be used as a base for a sauce. Be careful to check labels of tinned consommé as some contain sherry.

Quick Beef Stock

1 tin Campbell's Consommé diluted with ½ a tin of water
1 yellow onion, coarsely chopped
1 medium carrot, chopped
1 stick of celery, chopped
2 tsps chopped fresh parsley or 1 tsp dried
1 bay leaf
5 or 6 peppercorns
pinch of thyme (depending on the use of the sauce you may decide to omit this)
2 tbs tomato paste

Mix ingredients together and simmer for about an hour or until the vegetables are essentially cooked away. If you lose too much of the volume of your tinned consommé, add a bit more or some boiling water. Strain the mixture through a sieve lined with cheesecloth (unless you have a very fine sieve, and can do without the cheesecloth).

Makes 600 ml/1 pint of stock

Quick Chicken Stock

For use as a base for white sauce or chicken soup, a similar procedure can be followed using a chicken stock cube, made up with 600 ml/1 pint water and the onion, carrots, celery, parsley, and pepper but omitting the thyme, bay leaf, or tomato paste, unless of course you want the colour that tomato paste will give. Thereafter, the procedure is the same as for the beef stock.

Makes 800 ml/1 pint

Sumptuous Seafood

In the course of researching recipes for this book I found that more fish recipes have wine in them than any other kinds of dishes. Many of the fish recipes are quite complicated, involving many steps for poaching and for preparation of sauces. When you are working with this type of recipe, we suggest you go over it in advance, substituting fish stock, fish bouillon cubes, or half as much cider vinegar wherever white wine is called for. Where the main flavour of the poaching liquid is white wine, you can enhance the flavour of your nonalcoholic liquid with an onion, a carrot, a stick of celery, some parsley, and perhaps a peppercorn or two. This will provide an excellent poaching liquid even if you start with just plain water. Using the alcohol-based recipe as a master recipe, go through it before you begin and make these substitutions. We have done it for you throughout this book in order to give you an idea of our method. However, during my talks with various people it's become clear that they have many favourites they would like to use if they only knew how to convert the recipe to avoid the alcohol. It is our hope that by following our lead you will be able to return to your own special recipes and produce the results that may have confounded you in the past when facing the nonalcoholic entertainment blues.

Rich, creamy, and wine-free

Coquilles St. Jaques

450g/1 lb scallops
5 medium potatoes, sliced
½ medium carrot, diced
½ medium celery stick, chopped
2 large shallots
¾ kg/1½ lbs mushrooms, sliced
pinch of cayenne pepper
white pepper to taste
freshly ground black pepper
50 g/ 2 oz grated Gruyère, the Swiss cheese with the
   holes
15 g/½ oz butter
350 ml/12 fl oz skimmed milk
150 ml/¼ pint of double cream (optional)
2 medium tomatoes, peeled, seeded, chopped

Peel and slice potatoes, boil in plain water until tender. Pour off water, add black and cayenne pepper to taste, pour in some of the milk and beat until smooth but not so wet that peaks don't form. You may need more or less of the milk depending on the temperature and the amount of water in the air. Set, covered, on the back of the stove on warm. Melt the butter in a heavy enamel or stainless steel pan, add the mushrooms, and turn the heat up to high. Sauté the mushrooms until they give up most of their moisture, turn heat to simmer, remove the mushrooms to side bowl and add the chopped celery, carrot, and shallot to the pan. Cover and simmer for 15 minutes or until the vegetables are soft, but take care not to get the heat so high that they take on any colour. Add some additional water to the pan if you must in order to keep the vegetables cooking properly. When they are finished, return the mushrooms to the pan, cover, and cook for 10 more minutes. Add the scallops, cover, and check after 3 to 5 minutes, as the scallops cook very fast and you want a just-done scallop. When you get there take everything except the juice out of the pan, add the tomato, boil it and the juice down rapidly over high heat until it starts to crackle. Add cream and boil again until the sauce is slightly thickened. Meanwhile, preheat the grill, take an oven-proof gratin dish, or lacking that, any heavy metal frying pan, but don't use aluminium (or you can use a shallow casserole; anything that can take the grill heat). Pipe or spoon the potato around the edges, put the mushrooms and scallops in the centre and pour the sauce all over. Sprinkle cheese evenly over the whole surface and set it under the grill for a few minutes until it is lightly browned.

The fancy version of this is to pipe individual serving shells, which you can buy in most kitchenware shops, with the potato and then put the scallops in the centre of each individual shell, cover with the sauce, sprinkle with cheese and grill. To get the shells to sit up properly during grilling just place in a swiss-roll pan that's been sprinkled with coarse salt.

Serves six

Lobster Newberg without wine? Yes—they're just as wonderful when they're on the wagon.

Lobster Newberg

This recipe for Lobster Newberg has been worked out to retain the slightly nutlike flavour that you normally get when sherry is used to finish the sauce, but without the slightest hint of sherry or any other alcohol. This recipe's most essential ingredient is the cooked lobster meat. If you are cooking the lobsters yourself, make sure they're alive and well when you buy them. You can tell by having a look at their tails. A live lobster's tail is curved tightly in a 'C' shape, and if you can pull it open it snaps right back. If the lobster is the least bit limp or its tail is out flat, don't buy it. These days the claws are either pegged or kept closed with strong rubber bands and there is little danger of getting attacked by an irritable fellow. If you want to be sure that they don't get you before you get them, remand them to your refrigerator and, just before cooking, sneak up on 'em and pop them into the freezer for about 10 to 15 minutes. Getting them very cold pacifies the critters and makes it easier for you to handle them. This recipe calls for 2 lobsters, each weighing ½–¾ kg or 1¼–1½ lbs. You can save money by buying 'culls,' lobsters which may have lost a claw or some other piece of their anatomy. Since they ain't perfect, poor dears, they command a considerably lower price per pound than the whole ones with both claws attached. We use Northern-type lobster for the recipe although there's no reason why you can't use frozen lobster tails from the Southern 'spiny' lobster. If you use these, follow the directions on the box for cooking them. To prepare your lobsters, whether northern or southern, bring to the boil in a large pot:

600 ml/1 pint water
1 bay leaf
1 tsp thyme
10 peppercorns

4 parsley sprigs
1 medium carrot, chopped
1 medium onion, chopped
1 large stick of celery, chopped

Simmer this mixture for 10 minutes. Take the lobsters from the freezer and if the claws are handcuffed—or should we say clawcuffed—with rubber bands, cut through the bands and swiftly drop the critters into the pot before they get angry. Put the 2 of them in there together as nearly at the same time as possible, not for a jacuzzi romance, but so that the cooking time can be easily regulated. Allow the liquid to come back to the boil, and simmer for 20 to 25 minutes, depending on the size of the lobsters.

Mushrooms for Sauce

350 g/¾ lb fresh mushrooms, sliced
5 tbs water
1 tsp lemon juice

Simmer the mushrooms in the water and lemon juice for 15 minutes. Skim the mushrooms out of the water, squeeze lightly to get all the liquid out and set aside. When the lobsters are cooked, add mushroom liquid to the lobster liquid and cook it down until you have only 150 ml/¼ pint left. Strain and reserve. Taste. It may be too strong and require diluting.

While you've been doing the mushrooms, the lobsters will have been 'chilling out,' as the kids say these days. Remove the lobster meat from the shell and cut into bite-sized chunks, reserving some of the claws whole. Be sure to de-vein the lobster tail and, if the lobster is a large one, don't forget the meat in the side claws and in the flippers on the tail. Any roe and the green liver (tamale) should be removed and set aside to be served as side dishes. You should have about 350 g/12 oz.

Sauce

40 g/1½ oz butter
1 tbs grapeseed oil
3 egg yolks
225 ml/8 fl oz double cream (you can use a single cream if you're worried about the calories)
the reserved mushrooms
½ tsp paprika
50 ml/2 fl oz of the lobster liquid

Put the butter and oil in a heavy saucepan, add the lobster meat and stir until it's sizzling a bit, about 2 or 3 minutes. Add the reduced cooking liquid and cook for another minute or two. Lower the heat and add the paprika and mushrooms. Take the pan off the heat, beat egg yolks with the double cream (or single cream, bearing in mind that if you use single cream you won't get quite as heavy a sauce). Add the egg mixture to the lobster mixture off the heat, return pan to the stove and cook over low heat just until it's *about* to come to the boil. You don't want to boil this mixture as you'll get a lumpy sauce with little bits of cooked egg floating around in it. This sauce depends on the cream and the egg yolks for thickening—there's no other thickener in it to prevent this separation if you do boil it by accident. (If I've thoroughly scared you about your ability to produce this sauce without accidentally boiling it, one way out is to remove the lobster after sautéing it briefly in the butter and oil mixture. Then proceed with the rest of the sauce as per the original instructions. If you do inadvertently overcook it, you would then be able to smooth it out in a blender or a food processor and return it to the pot and add the lobster.) If you need to hold this dish for a short time, say from the beginning of the meal until it's time to serve it, place the pot with the completed lobster dish in another pot containing hot but *not boiling* water. The dish will then stay at serving temperature and you won't have to worry about cooking the egg by accident. Since this is a heavily egg yolk-laced dish, don't hold it for too long, particularly if it's out in the open at room temperature. (You want smiling guests, not ailing ones.) Also, don't cover it tightly if it's on the back burner as the steam from the cover could thin the sauce and ruin it. Just cover it partially to allow the steam to escape.

Serves two as main course, four as an appetizer

This delightful recipe is an alcohol-free version of Moules Marinières, a popular restaurant speciality that tends to be composed primarily of white wine.

Mussels in Sauce Without Wine

1½–1¾ kg/3½ lbs mussels
25–45 g/1–1½ oz unsalted butter
2 shallots, chopped
1 clove garlic, chopped
court bouillon reduced to 50 ml/2 fl oz
pepper (optional)

First, clean the mussels. If you are unfamiliar with handling mussels (or other bivalves such as clams), I recommend that you start off with a relatively small batch as they can be quite a bit of trouble until you get the hang of it. Here is an old New England method of making sure that not one grain of sand is served with your mussels or clams.

Get a bucket of sea water, or lacking that, salt some tap water. Plunge the mussels or clams into the water, and sprinkle the top of the water with a handful or two of yellow or white cornmeal. (You can use ordinary flour, but cornmeal works a bit better). Then lower a bubbler from a fish tank into the water and let the mussels sit and clean themselves for at least 4 to 5 hours (overnight if you have time). You need the bubbler to aerate the water enough so that they don't die from lack of oxygen. This is particularly true if you have a large batch of clams or mussels and they're rather tightly packed. This step is not absolutely necessary but it will guarantee no grains of sand in your dish. When you have finished cleaning them, take them out of the water and rinse them again. In the case of mussels, trim the beards and scrub them well with a wire brush or scrubbing cloth. Meanwhile, in a large frying pan with a top to it melt the unsalted butter and sauté the shallots and garlic until transparent. Add the court bouillon, turn up heat to medium-high, add mussels, cover pan, and shake it back and forth across the flame to keep the mussels moving around in the pan. Check the pan—the mussels are done when their shells are open and they have released all of their wonderful juices into the bottom of the pan. Taste the sauce before serving; you may want to add a bit of pepper at this point. This dish is served in soup bowls. It's traditional to leave a little bit of broth behind in case the cook missed any grains of sand when the mussels were cleaned.

Serves four

This recipe uses Plaice, which is a readily available, popular white fish that's suitable for serving in many ways. You'll need an ovenproof dish; I use a frying pan that has a metal handle and is fairly deep.

Poached Fish Fillets

1 kg/2 lbs plaice fillets
salt (optional)
white pepper
1 tbs shallots, chopped
—or—
2 tbs spring onions, chopped
1 tbs butter
300 ml/½ pint fish stock (this can be made from fish bouillon cubes, in which case don't add salt to the recipe)
50 ml/2 fl oz water
150 ml/¼ pint double cream (optional)

Pour in enough liquid to just cover the fish. If it looks as though you'll have more liquid than you need, hold back a bit on the water. Bring it to the simmer on the top of the stove, cover, and put into a preheated 180°C/350°F/Gas Mark 4 oven. Cook for 12 to 15 minutes or until the fish has turned opaquely white and flakes easily with a fork. Remove from the heat, remove fillets from the poaching liquid and, if you wish, cook the liquid down until it's reduced by about half, pour in the double cream and continue to boil until it reaches the desired consistency. This simple basic sauce can be used in many different ways.

Serves four

Beef and Poultry Entrées: Dining Without Wining

Unlike the traditional recipe, ours contains NO wine whatsoever and as a result has a slightly different but equally delightful taste.

Coq Au NO Vin

---

4 rashers bacon, diced (if you don't like the pork-salt taste, you may want to boil it for a few minutes in water to remove some of the salt)

2 tbs vegetable oil

1¼ kg/2½ lbs chicken, cut up

salt (optional)

½ tsp black pepper

600 ml/1 pint doctored beef stock (see recipes in the Soups and Stocks section)

225 ml/8 fl oz tomato juice or tomato-based vegetable juice (but be sure not to use Bloody Mary Mix)

1 tsp tomato paste

3 cloves garlic, minced

2 pinches thyme

1 bay leaf

40 g/1½ oz flour

40 g/1½ oz butter

In a heavy casserole cook the bacon very slowly until completely crisp; crumble and set aside. Add the oil to the fat in the casserole and turn the heat up until it's nice and hot, but not quite smoking; brown the chicken thoroughly. For better browning make sure your chicken's dry before it goes into the pot, as wet chicken simply is not going to give you the right colour. Since we aren't using red wine, careful browning of the chicken is crucial to achieving the colour you want in your sauce. Be extra careful not to scorch either the chicken or the pot, or you'll: a) ruin the sauce or b) have to wash out the casserole and start again. Sprinkle the pepper and, if you wish, salt, over the chicken, remove it, and pour out the excess fat. The importance of careful browning is to get the chicken nice and brown without burning it so that you have those beautiful browned juices for the sauce. Add the beef stock, tomato juice, tomato paste, garlic, thyme, and bay leaf and stir everything merrily around. Return the chicken to the liquid, cover the casserole, and bring it to simmer on the top of the stove. Then put it into a 180°C/350°F/Gas Mark 4 oven for about one hour. When the chicken is done, remove it from the casserole and let the liquid settle for a minute or two so the fat can rise to the top. Skim as much fat as possible off the top of the cooking liquid, remove the bay leaf, and bring it to a rapid boil over the highest possible heat. You want to reduce it to about 400 ml/¾ pint of liquid. In a separate pan, large enough to hold the liquid, melt the butter, and when it is foaming add the flour all at once. Stir over medium heat for a few minutes to remove the raw taste of the flour. Take the second pan off the heat and very, very slowly pour the reduced liquid in a stream into the flour and butter mixture. At first it will be very thick but as additional liquid is added it will thin out. If it doesn't seem thin enough, you can add a bit more stock (either beef or chicken). Return the pan to the heat and, stirring constantly, bring it to the boil. This will ensure a lovely smooth sauce even though it does use an extra pan.

Put the chicken in a deep serving dish (or back in the casserole if it can be used as a serving dish) and pour the sauce over the chicken. Sprinkle with the reserved bacon. Serve with buttered noodles and a crisp green vegetable.

Serves six

*Another chicken affair that almost always comes with wine or
some other spirit tucked away in the sauce is chicken breasts.
Chicken breasts are the basis of all kinds of marvellous dishes.
What I'm going to give you here is a very basic recipe with a
fundamental sauce. The variations are almost limitless. One of
my favourites is to cook fresh mushrooms with the chicken
breasts and then proceed with the sauce below. I allow 1 chicken
breast half for each light eater and 2 apiece for heavier eaters.
Try to get them about the same size so they will cook in the same
amount of time. There is nothing quite like overdone chicken
breasts for resembling India rubber.*

Chicken Breasts

6 chicken breast halves
juice of 1 lemon
salt (optional)
white pepper to taste
25 g/1 oz butter
150 ml/¼ pint beef stock or consommé
225 ml/8 fl oz whipping cream
black pepper
450 g/1 lb fresh mushrooms, sliced (optional)
2 tbs shallot, chopped
—or—
1 tbs onion, chopped

Remove any excess fat and any little flakes of bone from
the chicken breasts. Cover each with lemon juice and
white pepper. I like my chicken a little peppery so I use
about a teaspoon of white pepper for 6 chicken breast
halves. Melt the butter in your pan (I use a big frying pan
with a lid), add the chopped onion or shallot and cook for
a few minutes, until it starts to wilt a bit. Take the pan off

the heat, roll the chicken breasts (and mushrooms, if you're adding them) around in the butter, and arrange them in a circular shape in the pan—like pieces of pie. Cover and heat until it barely begins to simmer; then quickly pop it into a 190°C/375°F/Gas Mark 5 oven. Now you must watch very carefully. Test for doneness after about 10 minutes. The chicken breasts are cooked when they're no longer squishy to the touch. They need to be springy but not hard-springy as they tend to continue to cook for a few seconds after you take them out of the oven. If they are all nearly the same size they'll finish cooking at the same time—if some are springy while others are downright squishy, remove them individually in their own good time, putting them aside in a fairly deep dish with a little spout on the side. They always give out liquid and I like to incorporate this liquid into the sauce. You can also put them on a platter or in a pan and keep them, covered, on the back of the stove for warmth.

Meanwhile, take the cooking liquid the chicken has given out in the frying pan and add the beef stock, cooking it all down over high heat until it almost makes a syrup. You'll know you're getting there when the sound you hear changes from the bubble of a liquid to a kind of a cracking noise. If you just stick with your sauce, the first time you hear it you'll know. The minute that noise comes up, take the pan off the heat, pour in about 150–200 ml/¼–⅓ pint of cream, stir until it's mixed and then put the sauce back on the heat. Bring it to the boil and stay right there until the cream has thickened enough to make a nice white sauce. If you have used mushrooms it's not necessary to remove them. Let them stay right there and give their flavour out into the sauce. The last thing you do before you serve the sauce is to check the serving platter; if the chicken breasts have given out any juice, pour it into the sauce. If it waters the sauce too much, boil the sauce down a bit more, because you don't want to lose any of that great liquid. You then pour the sauce over the top of the chicken. If you want to be fancy and the chicken is in a grill proof dish, you can sprinkle either some cheddar or mixed cheddar and Swiss cheese on top and run it under the grill for a minute or two to give it a tasty browned cheese crust as a highlight.

Serves four to six

These can be served at a cocktail party or as a first course. As a main dish you cut back a bit on the spices to make it a little more bland.

Devilled Chicken Livers

225 ml/8 fl oz beef stock
50 ml/2 fl oz tomato juice (or tomato-based vegetable juice)
350 g/¾ lb chicken livers
350 g/¾ lb fresh mushrooms, cut into chunks
25 g/1 oz butter
2 tbs finely chopped shallots or onion
¼ tsp black pepper
salt to taste
1 tsp prepared Dijon mustard (use the kind that is
prepared *without* white wine)
2 tbs of the cooking liquid
2 tbs chopped parsley (for garnish)

Bring the beef stock and tomato juice to the boil in a saucepan, add the chicken livers and simmer for 5 minutes. Drain and reserve cooking liquid for the sauce. Chop livers into medium size chunks and set aside. Melt butter in the frying pan, add the cleaned, cut-up mushrooms and sauté them over high heat until they have given out their liquid and then reabsorbed it. Add the shallots, reduce the heat, and sauté them with the mushrooms; add the livers, pepper, and mustard. Add 2 tablespoons of the cooking liquid, and stir gently over medium-high heat to blend ingredients. When mixture is piping hot, remove to a heated serving dish, sprinkle with parsley, and serve immediately.

Serves two as main course, four as appetizer

Somehow our family has given the name 'Volleyballs' to this elegant dish. We also use the term to describe the whole recipe, which usually contains chicken in a cream sauce (often laced with white wine) and is served in pastry cases, which are the actual 'vol-au-vents.' Terminology aside, it's a lovely recipe with a number of interesting variations. It's delicious made with poached chicken breasts and also an excellent way to use up leftover chicken, turkey, or pheasant (duck or goose are too rich and too dark). At a pinch, you could substitute tuna fish, and tinned, cooked chicken may also be used.

Vol-au-Vents (Volleyballs)

2 whole chicken breasts, boned and halved
1 stick celery, chopped
1 small onion, chopped
1 small carrot, chopped
150 ml/¼ pint water or chicken stock
white pepper
lemon juice
salt (optional)

Season the chicken breasts (which will give you about 3 cups of cooked, diced meat) with white pepper and a few drops of lemon juice, adding salt only if you are accustomed to using it in cooking. Poach the celery, onion, and carrot in the water or chicken stock in a heavy frying pan until the vegetables are soft and most of the poaching liquid has evaporated. Remove the pan from the heat and roll the chicken breasts in the vegetable mixture. Cover them tightly with a lid or put a circle of wax paper over them and then cover tightly with tin foil. Return to simmering. The small amount of liquid left in the pan will be enough to get the breasts started; as they cook they will give out liquid of their own. Cook them gently for just 10 to 15 minutes. As soon as they feel springy to the touch, they are done. It may be necessary to turn them once during the cooking process but certainly not more than that. Chicken breasts can cook very, very quickly indeed and tend to toughen if overcooked. Remove from heat and allow to cool in the poaching liquid. Meanwhile, begin preparing the sauce in a large saucepan.

Sauce

> 50 g/2 oz butter
> 50 g/ 2 oz flour
> 600 ml/1 pint poaching liquid or chicken stock
> ½ cup chopped celery
> 1 small onion, chopped
> ¾ kg/1½ lb mushrooms, browned (see instructions)
> 1 sliced tinned pimento, drained
> white pepper

Melt the butter and when it starts to bubble slightly add the flour all at once. Cook and stir over low heat until smooth and slightly cooked—about 2 to 3 minutes. Remove from heat and slowly stir in the poaching liquid (no need to strain), from which the fat has been removed. Stir constantly until smooth. Return the mixture to the heat and cook and stir it until it comes to the boil and is thickened slightly.

Add the mushrooms to the sauce, add the diced chicken or turkey, celery, onion, and white pepper and cook over medium heat until the vegetables are cooked through. Just before serving, add the sliced, drained pimento.

No-Fat Sautéed Mushrooms for Sauce

> ¾ kg/1½ lb fresh mushrooms, quartered if small, sliced if large

Heat a frying pan over very high heat, add the sliced mushrooms, and shake and stir them as they begin to cook. You must watch the mushrooms constantly, stirring all the while. The mushrooms will 'squeak' at first, and then begin to give out their juices. Keep moving them around in the pan as the juices are given up and then reabsorbed, at which point you'll need to lower the heat until they are delicately browned.

Vol-au-Vent Cases

I use the frozen, prepared cases and bake them according to the instructions on the packet. When they are finished, remove them from the oven, take the little tops off, and scrape out all of the soft pastry from the inside of the shell. Replace the tops and return them to the oven (which has been turned off) to crisp. You must not leave the soft glop on the inside or it will make your whole pastry shell soft.

Variations:

● For a very rich sauce, substitute double cream for some or all of the chicken stock.

● If mushrooms or pimento are not on your list of favourite foods, try substituting sliced stuffed olives.

● The creamed chicken or turkey may be served on toast (with or without butter and with or without crusts), or over rice or mashed potatoes. For an attractive casserole for lunch or dinner, put a layer of mashed potatoes on the bottom of the casserole, fill it with chicken or turkey mixture and mound or pipe additional potatoes around the edge of the dish. Sprinkle a mixture of grated cheddar, swiss and parmesan cheeses and a dash of cayenne pepper over the turkey, potatoes—everything—and heat in a 180°C/350°F/Gas Mark 4 oven for about 25 minutes or until the potato starts to brown. If all it needs is browning, put it under the grill instead and watch it closely for 2 or 3 minutes.

Serves six

As with the Coq au NO Vin, we have not tried to duplicate the taste of beef burgundy. We found through personal experiment that this is not a pleasing sensation to the palates of most recovering alcoholics, and we avoid it. We have instead come up with a lovely brown sauce that makes an excellent alternative to the traditionally wine-laden variety.

Beef Burgundy

4 to 5 thin rashers streaky bacon
vegetable oil
1¼–1¾ kgs/2½–3 lbs stewing beef, cut into cubes
2 carrots, chopped
2 medium onions, chopped
salt (optional)
½ tsp pepper
40 g/1½ oz flour
1 litre/1¾ pints beef stock
225 ml/8 fl oz tomato juice or tomato-based vegetable juice
2 tbs tomato paste
3 cloves garlic, minced
2 pinches thyme
2 bay leaves

Sauté the bacon in a heavy casserole, render it very carefully and then set it aside for later use. Add oil if needed to cover the bottom of the casserole, and carefully brown each piece of beef on all sides, adjusting the heat so that you brown the beef without burning the fat in the pan, which can absolutely ruin the flavour of the dish. Put the beef aside in a bowl as it gets browned. When all of the beef is nicely browned, pour off the fat and put the meat back into the casserole, adding salt (if you wish), pepper, carrots, and onions; sprinkle the flour to coat everything. Put the casserole in a 200°C/400°F/Gas Mark 6 oven for about 8 minutes, stirring the mixture once during that period. Remove from the oven, add the beef stock, tomato juice, tomato paste, garlic thyme, and bay leaf, and stir while bringing it to simmering point on top of the stove. Cover and return to the oven which has been lowered to 180°C/350°F/Gas Mark 4. Simmer the mixture, making sure it bubbles very slowly for 3 to 4 hours, during which time a very rich brown sauce will form.

Accompanying vegetables:

  12 whole small onions
  8 medium carrots in chunks
  6 medium potatoes, halved
  450 g/1 lb mushroom caps

Our favourite vegetables for this particular dish are onions, carrots, potatoes, and mushrooms. If you want to be fancy, you can parboil the vegetables and sauté each of them separately just until they are lightly browned and glossy. (We do this in butter for a richer flavour.)

When the beef is tender, take it out of the casserole and strain the liquid into a pot, allowing it to sit briefly while the fat rises to the top. Meanwhile arrange the meat and all of those lovely vegetables in a presentation casserole. Skim absolutely all of the fat off the sauce; keep skimming as more of it rises. You can help this happen by putting it over a low heat for a few minutes. Check your sauce to see if it's thick enough to coat the spoon. If it is too thin, cook it down; if it's too thick, add some reserved beef stock. Once you get the sauce exactly where you want it, pour it over the arranged vegetables in the casserole.

Suggestions for preparing the vegetables separately: There is a trick to boiling the onions without having them fall apart: cut a little cross into the root end of the onions and drop them into boiling water for about 10 to 12 minutes. Fish them out and drain them with the root side up so that all of the water lodged in between the layers of the onion can drain out. Start the potatoes in cold water and boil for about 20 minutes; then drain thoroughly. Meanwhile in a big frying pan bring to foaming 25–50 g/1–2 oz of butter or a mixture of butter and oil. Starting with the parboiled carrots, roll the vegetables around in the frying pan until they are coated with butter and begin to form a little crust on them. If, when you put the onions in you increase the heat a bit, you begin to get browned onions (because of the sugar content). If you like them very brown, just keep 'em cooking a bit more—the longer, the browner. Then take the onions out, adding more butter or fat if necessary, and put the potatoes in. The drained potatoes will meanwhile have dried off and will absorb the butter to begin acquiring a crust of their own. Sauté the mushrooms according to the method described in Vol-au-Vents (Volleyballs).

Serves six

This is an adaptation of Belgium's famous Carbonnades à la Flamande, which uses beer instead of wine as the braising liquid. We recommend substituting nonalcoholic beer, which may make the results unacceptable to recovering alcoholics. If you plan to serve this to someone who might object to the use of a beer taste, we suggest that you check with them ahead of time to be sure that this is not the case. Because the small amount of alcohol that may be present in the beer will be completely cooked out, it is only a question of flavour. Using nonalcoholic beer does not, however, alter the taste of the sauce, which tastes exactly like the 'real thing.'

Braised Beef In 'Beer'

4 to 5 thin rashers of streaky bacon
2 tbs vegetable oil
1¼–1¾ kg/2½–3½ lbs stewing beef, cut into cubes
2 carrots, chopped
4 large onions, sliced
salt to taste (optional)
½ tsp pepper
40 g/1½ oz flour
400 ml/¾ pint nonalcoholic beer
400 ml/¾ pint beef stock
2 tbs tomato paste
3 cloves garlic, pressed
1 bay leaf

Stir the bacon in a large oven-proof casserole or pot over low to medium heat until most of the fat is cooked out and the bacon is crisp. Crumble and set aside. Add the oil to the casserole and, carefully regulating the heat, brown the meat on all sides. Add the carrots and onions to the casserole and brown them for several minutes. Remove the browned vegetables, pour out the extra fat, and return the browned meat to the casserole. Sprinkle the flour over the meat and put the casserole, uncovered, into a preheated 200°C/400°F/Gas Mark 6 oven for about 5 minutes, to form a crust on the meat. Remove the casserole and add the vegetables, stirring to mix. Add the beer and stock, garlic, salt, pepper, bay leaf, and tomato paste. Cover and bring to a simmer on the top of the stove. Move to the oven, which has been reduced to 180°C/350°F/Gas Mark 4, and cook for 3 to 4 hours. When done, pour off the liquid, let the fat rise to the top, and degrease it. It should be thick enough to use as is. If it is too thin, simmer until it thickens. If too thick, add some additional beef stock until it reaches the desired consistency. Serve with noodles and a lightly steamed green vegetable such as green beans or Brussel sprouts.

Serves six to eight

This is my favourite meat loaf. I'm including it in this book because it's so useful sliced cold as a coarse paté. Unlike most patés, it contains no alcohol and may be first served hot as a meat loaf and then the next day as a paté.

Meat Loaf

1 kg/2 lbs fresh lean ground beef
50 g/ 2 oz fine-textured unflavoured commercial bread crumbs
2 eggs, lightly beaten
1 × 455 g/16 oz tin tomatoes
⅓ of a large Spanish onion
—or—
1 medium onion, finely chopped
1 tsp salt (optional)
½ tsp ground black pepper
½ tsp celery seasoned salt
2 stalks of celery, finely chopped
3 bacon rashers (optional)

Place all of these ingredients in a large mixing bowl, mixing only enough to combine; don't overdo as it will toughen the meat. Pat gently into a casserole large enough to hold the mixture with room to spare. Mound it in the centre and pat it into a kind of a loaf shape or, if your casserole is round, into a pie shape, a little higher in the centre. Put 2 or 3 thinly-sliced bacon rashers across the top if you like and if necessary let the mixture stand until it reaches room temperature. Bake at 180°C/350°F/ Gas Mark 4 for 45 minutes to 1 hour. After removing from the oven let it stand at the back of the stove for 30 to 45 minutes before cutting to allow the meat to take up some of the moisture from the pan. If serving as meat loaf, simply warm it up a bit if necessary and cut it right from the pan and serve. If it's to play the role of paté, drain the pan of all excess liquid, put the liquid in a container and allow the fat to rise to the top, discarding all of the excess fat. Pour the remaining liquid back into the pan with the meat loaf, cover it closely and refrigerate. Just before introducing it as a paté, take it out of the refrigerator and, while it's still quite cold, slice it thinly or into individual bites and serve at room temperature with sliced egg and/or onion, gherkin pickles, and small lettuce leaves as garnish.

Serves Six

Assorted Specialities

Here's a nice recipe for fruit and yogurt to take the place of the fruit compôtes (Uncle Harry calls them fruit composts) so often laden with alcohol.

Fruit and Yogurt

---

225 ml/8 fl oz plain yogurt
2 tbs honey
½ tsp nutmeg
1 tbs frozen concentrated orange juice
sliced almonds, toasted

Fill half a cantaloupe-type melon with a mixture of whatever fresh fruit you have on hand (sliced cherries, plums, nectarines, or whatever) plus some sliced banana. Mix the yogurt with the honey, nutmeg, and juice, and cover the fruit, sprinkling the top with sliced almonds.

Serves two

Fruit Cup

Squeeze the juice of a lemon or lime over the slices, cubes, or balls of fruit and then douse with sparkling apple juice or very dry ginger ale. A dash of cinnamon, nutmeg, or allspice adds interest.

This is an excellent savoury to serve either at the beginning of a meal or, if you are doing a very formal dinner, at the very end after the sweet. (This is when you would normally serve Port but a rich, red grape juice would also be a good accompaniment.) I don't recommend mushroom toast for tea as it's a bit greasy and drippy and I don't think your guests would be comfortable walking around with it on tea plates.

Mushroom Toast

450 g/1 lb fresh mushrooms
1 medium onion or 2 shallots, finely chopped
25 g/1 oz butter
1 tsp pepper (or to taste)
salt to taste
butter for toast slices

First cut the crusts off and toast whatever bread you have on hand. (Wheat, white, rye; fresh or slightly stale—the mushrooms go with just about everything.)

Try to get small mushrooms so that you can use the caps whole. If that's not possible, chop them or slice thinly. The mushrooms will be sautéed separately. Bring the butter to foaming in a sauté pan, add the mushrooms, turn the heat up high and toss the mushrooms around in the pan; they will give out their liquid and then take it back up again. When they've gone through this whole process, continue to cook them until they're brown. Add a good teaspoon of black pepper per pound/450 g of mushrooms. You want this dish to be a little bit spicy. Add salt to taste and, toward the end, after you've turned the heat down on the mushrooms, add the finely chopped shallots or onion to sauté with the mushrooms. (You can't put the onion in first or it will burn; it contains too much sugar to allow it to withstand the very high heat that mushrooms can.)

Lightly butter both sides of each piece of toast, take the mushrooms out of the frying pan, and fry the toast in the pan until it forms a nice, crispy exterior. Arrange the mushrooms on the toast in patterns, either buttons or layers or slices or a spreading of chopped pieces, and sprinkle a bit of butter over the top of each separate slice of toast. Put the slices on a baking sheet or grill pan. When you are ready to serve, grill just until the tops of the mushrooms are bubbling and brown. Serve the mushroom toast immediately on warmed plates, as it can lose its heat very quickly. (I sometimes sprinkle them lightly with freshly grated parmesan for cheese aficionados.)

Serves six

Cucumbers can be beautiful

Green Cucumber Mousse

75 g/3 oz lime jelly
225 ml/8 fl oz boiling water
1 tbs vinegar
¼ tsp salt (optional)
½ cucumber, chopped and seeded
150 ml/¼ pint sour cream
150 ml/¼ pint mayonnaise
1 tsp minced onions

Dilute jelly with water according to directions on packet, stir in the vinegar and salt and let partially set. When it gets to the gloppy stage, fold in the other ingredients; mould and let set until firm.

Serves four

No brandy, no sherry, just lots of flavour.

Duck or Chicken Liver Paté

450 g/1 lb duck or chicken livers (duck livers are richer, if you can get them)
225 g/½ lb butter
1 medium onion, coarsely chopped
Salt and pepper to taste
¼ tsp nutmeg
½ tsp thyme
150 ml/¼ pint strong chicken stock (If you use chicken stock made with cubes and salted butter do not add salt to this recipe until you have tasted it.)

Sauté onions and livers in 50 g/2 oz of the butter, add the remaining ingredients and cook until the liquid is reduced to 50 ml/2 fl oz. For this recipe you want to cook the livers nearly all the way through. Meanwhile, melt the rest of the butter and set aside. When the livers are cooked, pour the melted butter into a food processor or blender. Then add the liver mixture and blend thoroughly until smooth. At this point taste for salt and if necessary, correct the seasoning. Pour it into a crock or a glass bowl—DO NOT USE ALUMINIUM. Cover it and chill.

This paté will not stand up alone very well but it will always spread consistently, even when chilled. Be sure to cover the bowl before you refrigerate it so that the paté doesn't form a skin!

Serves four

Apple juice replaces apple brandy in these delicious

Roquefort Almond Balls

100 g/4 oz Roquefort cheese
100 g/4 oz cream cheese
2 dashes tabasco
100 g/4 oz toasted almonds, chopped
1 tbs chives, finely chopped
1 tbs apple juice

Let the cheese soften to room temperature and, in a blender or food processor, blend in the apple juice and tabasco. Remove and stir in a third of the almonds and all of the chives. Chill for a few hours or overnight. Form into balls and roll in the remaining almonds.

Makes about 16 balls (or can be rolled into one big ball for 8 people).

A delectable large-party side dish

Bacon, Noodle, Cheese, and Tomato Casserole

450 g/1 lb egg noodles, cooked al dente
2 × 454 g/16 oz tins tomatoes
225 g/½ lb cheddar cheese, grated
4 thin rashers smoked streaky bacon

Cook the noodles al dente according to packet directions. (If there are no directions, subtract about 3 minutes from the recommended time on the packet.) Since they will be baked after assembly, you want them slightly under-done. Drain, rinse in cold water, drain again, and put ⅓ of the noodles in the bottom of a large buttered casserole (I use a 12″/135 cm round casserole that is 4″/10 cms deep). Spread 1 can of the stewed tomatoes over the noodles and top with ⅓ of the cheese. Make a second layer with the second ⅓ of the noodles, the second tin of tomatoes, and the second ⅓ of the cheese. Add the last ⅓ of the noodles and the last ⅓ of the cheese. Lay the four strips of bacon across the top to make 'stripes' on the surface. Bake in a preheated 180°C/350°F/ Gas Mark 4 oven for 45 minutes. Remove from the oven, let settle for about 10 minutes, and serve. This dish can be kept hot over warming candles, but is tasty even when lukewarm.

Serves ten or more

Traditional fondue is highly alcoholic and cannot be served to recovering alcoholics because the cooking does not remove the alcohol. In fact, most people can taste the underlying wine and kirsch in the recipe. Our version produces an excellent fondue with a true Swiss cheese taste, but no hint of any type of alcohol; we make it with milk. Yes, milk!

Cheese Fondue

300 ml/½ pint milk (skimmed milk may be used)
100 g/4 oz Emmenthal cheese
100 g/4 oz Gruyère cheese
25 g/1 oz flour
1 large clove garlic, quartered
black pepper and nutmeg to taste
bread for dipping

If you don't have the traditional fondue pot, it's easy to make this dish on the stove in a saucepan. Just remember to keep the heat medium-low so that you don't scorch any of the ingredients. Once you have done the basic mixing on the stove, you can bring it to the table and put it over 3 warming candles grouped together. It's an excellent way to use leftover French or Italian bread. The slightly stale diced bread that is customarily dipped into cheese fondue should be crusty as it will soften a bit as you immerse it in the fondue. Cut it so that each piece has a portion of crust. You will need long forks for dipping and ordinary forks for eating.

Grate the cheese, put it into a plastic bag, and set it aside. Rub a stainless steel or enamel saucepan with a cut clove of garlic.

Heat the milk in the fondue pot or saucepan to simmering point, uncovered. Add the pieces of garlic to the milk if you like a stronger garlic taste and leave it in the mixture until just before you serve it.

Sprinkle the flour over the grated cheese, close the bag, and shake it until the flour coats each piece of cheese. This step is essential; it will keep your fondue from separating. As the milk comes to the boil, add the grated cheese gradually, tipping it out of the bag while stirring constantly. At this point you must watch the dish. If you walk away from the stove and stop stirring, you risk lumps and bumps and possibly some boiling milk. Adjust the heat so that it's just high enough to keep it barely under the boil and continue to add the cheese and flour

mixture, stirring to keep it smooth. It will thicken as you add the cheese. When about one-third of the cheese has been added, you'll notice a change in texture. As you stir, add a bit of nutmeg if you like the taste, and two generous shakes of ground black pepper. (If you prefer to use white pepper, use less as it is hotter than black pepper.) When the fondue begins to bubble, move the pan from the stove to the warmer on the table, where everyone can enjoy dipping the bread, swirling it through the fondue, and removing it to individual plates to eat with separate forks. (Don't try to eat the bread from the dipping fork; a) it's unhygienic, and b) you may burn your mouth.) This recipe does not lend itself readily to reheating. It will retain its nice taste, but its smooth texture becomes slightly grainy and you may need to add extra milk to return it to dipping consistency.

Serves two as main course, four as appetizer

The savoury recipe for these, with the filling of your choice, makes a lovely light luncheon dish. It's also an intriguing—and very tasty—solution to what to do with leftover Chinese food. The sweet version is the basis for our alcohol-free Crêpes Suzette, which appear in the dessert section.

Egg Crêpes

For each 2 to 3 crêpes use:
   1 egg
   1 tsp water
   1 tsp flour
   1 tsp milk
   1 pinch of salt
For savoury crêpes add:
   1 teaspoon finely grated onion
   pinch of garlic powder
   salt and pepper to taste
For sweet crêpes add:
   ¼ teaspoon sugar

To sauté use: ½ teaspoon butter for each crêpe. Blend desired ingredients well. Refrigerate for an hour or two or until mixture is completely smooth. Melt butter to foaming in medium-hot crêpe pan or small frying pan. Add enough crêpe batter to thinly cover bottom of pan, tilting to distribute evenly. Cook quickly on both sides; turn crêpe by flipping in pan or place dish over pan, turn pan over, and slide crêpe back into pan to cook briefly.

When crêpes are cooked ahead of time, they may be stored in the refrigerator with a piece of waxed paper between each crêpe. Allow to come to room temperature before attempting to separate.

These crêpes are suitable for use with our Crêpes

Suzette recipe or may be filled with any sweet filling.

Fillings:

For each savoury crêpe use:
    3 or 4 stalks freshly cooked asparagus
    1 tbs Gruyère cheese, grated
    1 tbs cheddar cheese, grated
    1 tbs Parmesan or Romano cheese, grated
    dash of cayenne

Mix Gruyère and cheddar cheeses with cayenne: sprinkle over asparagus. Roll crêpe over asparagus mixture and top with grated Parmesan or Romano cheese. Bake in 180°C/350°F/Gas Mark 4 oven for 10 minutes or until heated through and cheese is melted; brown top under preheated grill if desired.

For each savoury crêpe use:
    3 to 4 mushrooms, sautéed until juices are absorbed
    1 tablespoon sour cream (or yoghurt or blended cottage cheese)
    pinch basil
    pinch marjoram
    salt and pepper to taste

Savoury Sauces, Gravies, Marinades

This excellent low-calorie curry sauce can be used in place of curry mayonnaise with cold fish.

Cold Curry Sauce

---

225 g/8 oz low-fat cottage cheese or 'Quark'
1 tsp mild curry powder
1 tbs chopped shallot
1 tsp honey
1½ tsps lemon or lime juice
⅛ tsp ground ginger, if you wish

Put the low-fat cottage cheese in the blender or food processor. Add the shallot and blend until all of the lumps are gone. This can take a minute or two, but if you're doing it in a blender, flip it on and off and you won't liquefy it by accident. Then add all of the other ingredients, except for the last ½ teaspoon of lemon or lime juice, and blend until well-mixed. Taste, and if you need a little more sharpness, add the remaining lemon or lime juice. Cover and refrigerate for 4 hours or overnight.

Makes about 300 ml/½ pint

These marinades are listed with the meats and poultry with which they work best and, for a change, do not involve alcohol.

Marinade 1: For Lamb or Beef

    2 cloves garlic
    1 tsp crushed rosemary
    1 tbs Pommery mustard
    1 tbs soy sauce
    150ml/¼ pint olive oil

Press the garlic cloves or mash them with the flat side of a heavy knife. Put in a glass dish or a large cup, add the remaining ingredients, and stir it all up. This may be stored for a day or two if you wish. My preference is to make it a bit ahead as I like the garlicky flavour it acquires. The night before you plan to roast the meat, rub the mixture all over the outside of the meat or, if you are preparing lamb chops, put them in a glass dish and pour it over them, turning the chops so that they are thoroughly covered. Refrigerate overnight. The next day take the meat out and let it warm to room temperature. Remove any excess oil from the outside of the roast with paper towels, and thoroughly drain and blot the chops with the towels before cooking.

Makes about 150 ml/¼ pint

Marinade 2: For All Kinds of Poultry, Including Duck, and for Lamb and Pork

2 tbs sugar
300ml/½ pint freshly squeezed orange juice
2 tbs distilled white vinegar
2 tsps lemon juice
1 tsp lime juice
½ tsp dry mustard
If you are using it for beef or lamb add:
2 beef bouillon cubes
If you are using it for chicken or pork add:
2 chicken bouillon cubes
Salt and pepper to taste
3 tbs chopped fresh basil

Massage the salt and pepper into the meat (salt is optional). In a heavy saucepan cook and stir the sugar over low heat until it takes on a light caramel colour. Off the heat, very gradually, add the orange juice. The sugar may be so hot that the juice splatters so add it very, very carefully. Stir this until the sugar dissolves, then add the vinegar. If necessary return it to the heat a bit to make sure the sugar dissolves completely. If you have overdone the sugar—made it a very dark colour instead of a nice light caramel colour—discard the whole thing and start all over again or your marinade will have a burned taste. Cool the sugar/orange juice/vinegar mixture and when cool add the lemon juice, lime juice, and the dry mustard. Put in a glass bowl, add the meat, turning it over in the marinade, and refrigerate overnight. The next day drain the meat and pat it dry. It is now ready to roast or barbecue, as you prefer.

You may also use the marinade as the base for a sauce.

Add the beef or chicken bouillon to the reserved marinade and cook over medium heat until the liquid is reduced by about half. Allow plenty of time for this, especially if you are using a normal stove. It may take 15 to 20 minutes. Reduce the heat and if you want a rich sauce, add about 150ml/¼ pint double cream. Bring the sauce back to the boil and cook for just a few minutes, until the cream thickens. This sauce is an excellent accompaniment to meat, but does have a slightly sweet taste because of the orange juice, which you will want to take into consideration.

Makes about 450 ml/¾ pint

Marinade 3: For Lamb

> 75 ml/3 fl oz red grape juice
> 50 ml/2 fl oz vinegar
> 75 ml/3 fl oz olive oil
> 2 tsps fresh parsley, or 1 tsp dried
> ¼ tsp thyme
> 2 bay leaves
> 3 cloves garlic, crushed
> 1 tsp salt
> pinch of cayenne pepper

Mix ingredients together, spread the marinade over the meat (it can be used with any cut of lamb), cover, and marinate in the refrigerator several hours or overnight.

Makes about 225 ml/8 fl oz

Marinade 4: For Chicken or Small Game Birds

75 ml/3 fl oz olive oil
150 ml/¼ pint white grape juice
2 shallots, minced
1 clove garlic, chopped
1 small white onion, chopped
2 stalks of celery, chopped finely
½ tsp salt
½ tsp white pepper
¼ tsp ground rosemary

Mix ingredients together and spread over the poultry; refrigerate, covered, overnight. Open at least once to turn pieces to marinate evenly.

Makes about 450 ml/¾ pint

This is a super-good sauce to use with any poached fish or shellfish. It can be spiced up with additional herbs or mustard if you plan to use it with a strongly flavoured fish such as salmon.

Rich Sauce for Shellfish

100 g/4 oz butter
1 tbs shallots, finely chopped
50 ml/2 fl oz fish stock or poaching liquid
4 egg yolks
225 ml/8 fl oz double cream

Melt the butter in a saucepan and cook shallots until transparent. Add the fish stock or poaching liquid from cooked shellfish and cook for 3 to 4 minutes more. Meanwhile, beat the egg yolks and cream together until they are completely smooth. Over low heat, add the cream and egg mixture to the butter mixture in the saucepan and stir just until it thickens. Do not allow this sauce to boil or you'll end up with a scrambled-egg look. If, however, the unthinkable happens and you get scrambled eggs, a minute or two in the blender or food processor will correct the lumps. It will also thin your sauce out just a bit, and deprive it of its wonderful puffy texture, so do be cautious.

Makes about 600 ml/1 pint

Much has been said lately about finding spirits or wine in salad dressings. It's a mystery to me why anyone would make a point of adding wine to dressings, but it is indeed true, as I have discovered in many restaurants in the last few months. My vinaigrette dressing is a lemon vinaigrette but may also be made by substituting white distilled vinegar for the lemon juice.

Salad Dressings

I like to put the following ingredients in a fairly large screw-top jar:

1 tsp black pepper

A shake or two of garlic powder or one clove of minced garlic

A dash of dried mustard

(just under ½ teaspoon)

¼ tsp chervil

¼ tsp basil

salt (optional, and I usually leave it out)

Juice of 1 lemon

Cap the jar and shake it all up. Then fill the jar with 3 parts sunflower oil, 2 parts lemon juice and 1 part virgin olive oil. Cap the jar and shake it again. Taste it, and if it seems to need more oil, add a bit more. If it tastes 'sharp' enough, leave it alone because as the herbs soak into the dressing they become much stronger. This dressing takes refrigeration very well and can be used over the course of a week or so. Unless you like a strong garlic flavour, I think it's best to take the garlic out after the first few days. Exactly the same dressing may be made by substituting distilled white vinegar for the lemon juice or by using a combination of vinegars and including a little balsamic vinegar to give the dressing a slightly darker colour. The proportions are roughly the same; 1 part vinegar to 2 parts oil.

The plain vinaigrette sauce can become the base for an excellent blue cheese dressing: crumble blue cheese into a dish, pour the dressing over it, whipping it with a fork as you go. This is especially good over cos lettuce.

It was interesting to me to discover how many cooks put wine in their Italian tomato sauce. Here is a terrific, wineless, and very easy tomato sauce base which can be used for any kind of tomato-based pasta sauce. Once you've made a batch of this stuff, you can freeze some of it, and later add meat, mushrooms, sausage, or whatever you like. This sauce comes from a friend who is obviously not allergic to garlic.

Tomato Sauce Base

3 × 397 g/14 oz tins peeled Italian plum tomatoes, packed in tomato sauce
1 whole head of garlic, peeled and coarsely chopped
freshly ground black pepper
1 onion, finely chopped
1 bay leaf
1 tbs oregano
1 tsp basil
1 tsp olive oil
1 tsp sugar or honey or raisins (optional)

Put the tomatoes into a large pot, which should also be fairly heavy as this recipe requires hours of cooking. Add the onion, garlic, and seasonings, put the pot on the back of stove and start it simmering. From time to time stir it up, crushing the tomatoes as you go. This produces a sauce with a nice texture to it because the tomatoes never break up totally—little chunks of tomato are left in the sauce. This sauce should be simmered for at least 4 hours. I keep it mostly covered, just cracking the lid to let some of the steam escape, and stir it, stir it, stir it. After about 4 hours, I taste it, take a look at it to see if I like the texture, and if it's too thin, simmer it a little longer with the lid off. If it's too thick, I add a bit of hot water, but that happens very rarely. This is the basic spaghetti/pasta sauce. If you want to make a meat sauce, sauté the hamburger and/or Italian sausage separately and combine it with the sauce. If you like a mushroom sauce, add the mushrooms during the last 2 hours of cooking.

Serves six

Because this sauce often accompanies a beef roast, the de-greased pan drippings can also be added to it. If this makes the sauce too thin, simmer until it reaches the proper consistency.

Truffle Sauce

1 × 200–225 g/7–8 oz tin truffles plus liquid
25 g/1 oz flour
150 ml/¼ pint tinned beef consommé
1 tsp Bovril
2 tbs tomato paste
300 ml/½ pint chicken stock

Combine the flour with 2 tablespoons of the cold consommé and stir it into the blended chicken stock, Bovril, tomato paste and (if used) pan drippings. Bring to the boil, stir, reduce heat, and simmer until thickened. Then stir in the truffles with their sauce.

Makes about 450 ml/¾ pint

Tea For Two—or Twenty

This is a basic construction project consisting of a chef's version of a carpenter's creation—with sawing, scraping, pasting, hammering, plastering, painting, and finishing, except that the wood translates in to planks of bread, the plaster to fillings, the saw (or plane) to a serrated knife, the paint to icing, and the 'finishing' becomes decorating with colourful vegetables. You 'hammer' with the flat of your hand, gently, with love. The result: a really elegant tea party.

Fancy Tea Sandwiches

Okay. Ready? Hard hats on! Serrated knife in hand! Let's splurge with different kinds of bread loaves, unsliced, which we're going to integrate—wholemeal, rye, white, whatever. (It's fun to mix and match white and, let's say, wholemeal sandwiches when we're finished and ready to serve.) Unless it's a crusty country tea, 'plane' the crusts off the loaves; then 'saw' each loaf into three or four lengthwise 'planks.' Butter the inside surfaces of each and fill with any salad or whatever filling you have on hand, bearing in mind that should you have more than one kind of filling (and you should) they should be compatible when you serve them. 'Spackle' (spread, if you're not in the mood to play painter with us) the inside surfaces of the planks of bread with the filling, reassemble the loaves, tap-tap, pat-pat, wrap 'em in moist towels and chill 'em well, at least a couple of hours. Then remove them from the refrigerator and plaster them with softened cream cheese, just like icing a cake. You soften with mayonnaise or a little milk or cream so that it spreads—that's right—just like plaster. (I don't know

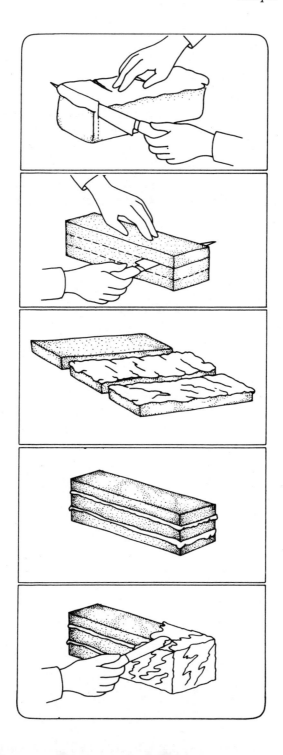

what they call it, there must be a term, I'm sure.) You artistic types who can't leave well enough alone might put a little pimento in it for a special marbleized pink colour. Finish the surfaces of the loaves with whatever pretty things you happen to have on hand, like sliced olive or sliced egg, or tiny radish roses with green pepper 'leaves,' or carrot curls, or whole black olives, or whatever sounds like fun. It's *your* construction project, after all. Now for the unveiling of your own special masterpiece: slice it down just like a loaf of cake so that it sections off like finger sandwiches when served.

There are so many wonderful ways to serve popovers! I like to substitute them for Yorkshire pudding with roast beef as nearly everyone likes them better. They are also delicious at brunch or breakfast, when their novelty can take the place of other dishes that might be served with alcohol. At dinner they can be either a case for a creamed dish or split open and filled with something rich and gooey for dessert. This is a very easy recipe; you do, however, need a blender to prepare it.

* Popovers

225 ml/8 fl oz milk
2 whole eggs (large)
15 g/½ oz soft butter
200 g/7 oz sifted S.R. flour
¼ tsp salt if pastry is to be used for savoury
—or—
¼ tsp sugar if pastry is to be used for sweet

Put all ingredients in a blender, cover, mix at low speed for 15 seconds. Preheat greased popover tins in a 220°C/425°F/Gas Mark 7 oven for a few minutes; pour in batter (fill to about the two-thirds mark). Bake approximately 40 minutes (absolutely *no* peeking—they can collapse and look hideous) or until they are puffed and brown.

There are several tricks to getting these things to puff up properly. First of all, be sure your oven is all the way up to 220°C/425°F/Gas Mark 7 and that it is thoroughly preheated. If you think the oven is running a bit slow, check the temperature as it won't work if it's not hot enough. You must have the deep popover (or baba au rhum) pan in order to get the popovers to pop. An

Editor's Note
Popovers are quite definitely American—they are also extremely good. The author's directions seem very clear. The only problem is to find the correct receptacles in which to make them. We suggest custard cups if you can't find baba-au-rhum tins.

ordinary cupcake pan will not work. The greasing of the tins should be done with melted butter or drippings and you should be generous—grease them all the way up the sides so the popovers can slip up as they puff. At the end of the cooking period when they're obviously puffed and golden brown, remove them from the oven and slit the side of the top with a sharp knife (just plunge the knife into the popover) and then return the popovers to the oven for about 5 minutes. The oven can be turned off at this point as soon as you get the popovers in and the oven door closed. This allows the steam to escape and keeps the popovers from becoming soggy.

Makes 8

Popover Variations:

If you want to use them in lieu of Yorkshire pudding, use a tablespoon of drippings from your roast pan instead of a tablespoon of soft butter; grease the tins generously.

If they are to be used as a case for a creamed dish of any sort, omit the sugar and just use the salt.

If you want to use them as a case for dessert, omit the salt and use the sugar.

This batch of tea sandwiches uses commercially prepared fill-
ings, which can be an absolute godsend when you are in a rush,
especially when they are doctored slightly so that they don't taste
as if they've just come out of a tin.

Tea Sandwiches

Start with a loaf of party pumpernickel or any good dark
bread. Spread one side of each slice thickly with liver
sausage, the other with mayonnaise, press the sandwiches together, cut them, and cover them quickly. This
type of dark bread dries out really fast and won't be
nearly as tasty if it gets that aged, dry look. (To keep the
sandwiches moist for a short time, you can wring out a
dishtowel until it's slightly damp and wrap the sandwiches in it. They can then be safely refrigerated for
several hours, in time to make their debut from the
dishtowel wrap tasting as though you have just made
them. Be careful not to get the dishtowel too wet or
you'll have soggy debutantes.)

Next, slit commercially prepared finger rolls—the
kind available in most supermarkets—lengthwise top to
bottom (whether oval-shaped or rectangular). Don't cut
them all the way through; you want to keep the two
halves from sliding about. Mix any commercially prepared chicken spread (*not* a chicken *liver* spread but a
general chicken spread) with a little bit of paprika and
chopped parsley, and a teeny-weeny bit of chopped
sweet pickle. (I wouldn't use more than a tablespoon of
the pickle mixture for an ordinary sized jar of the chicken
spread.) Fill the rolls with the spread. If you have to wait
a long time before they're to be eaten, don't add lettuce; if
they're going to be grabbed immediately, lettuce across
the top gives some lovely additional crunch to the sandwiches. Because these rolls have crust all around to keep
them moist, you can simply return them to the trays in

which they arrived and cover them snugly with plastic. They'll survive quite nicely for a number of hours in the refrigerator.

For the next group you need a package of round soft rolls, sliced part way through so that you have a little clam-shell hinge on the back. Fill these with prepared ham spread mixed with chopped onion, celery, and a little mayonnaise. If you plan to use them immediately it's okay to add lettuce; otherwise refrigerate them as is. In each case take the sandwiches out of the refrigerator early enough so that they can return to a cool room temperature before serving. These fillings definitely taste better at room temperature.

Here's to Good Friends—
and Zero-Proof Drinks

This recipe can be done nicely with nonalcoholic champagne. Because this does contain some alcohol (both in the bitters and a small amount in the non-alcoholic champagne), it should not be served to any recovering alcoholic.

Champagne Cocktail

small sugar cubes
Angostura Bitters
orange juice
orange slices
nonalcoholic champagne
fresh strawberries (optional)

Soak the sugar cube in the Angostura Bitters until about half of it has absorbed the colour of the bitters, put it in the bottom of a champagne glass, and pour a tiny bit of orange juice over it, at most a half-teaspoon. Fill the glass carefully with nonalcoholic champagne (don't shake it around too much because the sugar will cause it to foam up). Then add half of an orange slice (seeds removed) to the glass. A fresh strawberry will give it an elegant final touch.

Serves one

This bountiful recipe for Christmas Punch is also a perennial favourite at my New Year's Eve Party. It will spread cheer through a crowd of anywhere from 30 to 40 guests for an entire evening.

Christmas Punch

4 litres/6½ pints water

2 kg/4.5 lbs sugar

4½ kgs/10 lbs fresh or frozen strawberries (without sugar)

900 ml/1½ pints peach juice (or apricot)

450 ml/¾ pint freshly squeezed orange juice

225 ml/8 fl oz freshly squeezed lemon juice

7½ litres/4½ pints soda water

3 litres/5 pints soda water, frozen into cubes

Boil the water and sugar together, taking care to wash down the sides of the pan so that no crystals remain. Boil the mixture for 5 minutes, until it forms sugar syrup. Cool and set aside. (You may use all of it, some of it, or none, depending on how sweet you want your punch). Meanwhile, put the 3 litres of soda water in ice cube trays to freeze. (Ice cubes made from soda water will keep the punch sparkling without diluting it as the ice melts.)

Pour the peach/apricot juice, orange juice and lemon juice into your largest mixing bowl or a big pot. As you stir it together, begin adding sugar syrup until you get a very, very strong sweet/sour flavour. You must make this base syrup strong in order for it to stand up against being cut with all of that sodawater. When it reaches the point where it's strong enough and yet still carries the undertaste of the sharpness of the lemon, stop adding the sugar syrup and set it aside in case you need to use it later in the evening. Then pour this mixture into 1 litre bottles (which I reserve over the year for just this purpose) and refrigerate. This can be done the day before the party as it doesn't offend this juice mixture at all to sit for a day or so. The night of the party, pour one bottle of the base mixture into your punch bowl, add a generous amount of ice, and fill the punch bowl with soda water (about a bottle and a half or 2 bottles to each litre of base mixture). Float at least 1 kg/2 lbs of strawberries atop the punch for a buoyant decoration and watch your guests dive for it.

Serves thirty to forty

Mulled apple juice (still and fresh if possible) is a favourite in our house when autumn arrives. You will need the following spices for every 4 litres/7 pints of juice:
    8 whole allspice
    8 whole cloves
    4 sticks cinnamon (3"/18 cm long)
Depending on the sweetness of the apple juice you will probably want to add some brown sugar. This should be done as it is warming, to taste.

Mulled Apple Juice

Add the spices to the juice and bring to the simmer on the back of the stove; keep the heat regulated to just under a simmer so that the juice does not evaporate too much, and let it work for an hour or so. At this point, turn the heat down very low (just to keep it warm) and it's ready to be strained and served.

We serve this together with such other traditional (alcoholic) offerings as wine or champagne. The mulled juice always goes first, whether or not the crowd contains drinkers.

Serves eight

I make this recipe with vanilla essence because it will be cooked. Since you don't bring the mixture to a boil, some people might be concerned about the vanilla not cooking out (that 35-percent alcohol takes some removing); it can be made just as easily with vanilla bean or with vanilla sugar or fructose. You can also use the vanilla syrup described in The Vanilla Dilemma, being careful to cut back a bit on the sugar. This recipe isn't good if it gets too sweet, but it does depend on a strong vanilla flavour to be interesting.

Nonalcoholic Eggnog . . . and Syllabub

400 ml/¾ pint milk

50 g/2 oz sugar

3 egg yolks

1 tsp vanilla essence (or 1 teaspoon frozen vanilla or 1 teaspoon vanilla syrup and 1 teaspoon less of sugar)

150 ml/¼ pint double cream

nutmeg to taste

Scald milk. If you are using the vanilla bean method, put a vanilla bean in the milk while you are bringing it to a scald. Beat the sugar into the egg yolks until they're a light lemon colour, and if you are using vanilla essence, add it at that point, otherwise omit.

Pouring in a continuous stream and beating constantly, pour the scalding milk over the egg yolk/sugar mixture. Return the mixture to a saucepan and put over low heat. Cook and stir until it is slightly thickened but be careful not to bring to the boil. Cool the mixture and then chill. If you do heat this a little too much and too fast you'll get a change in texture with a kind of 'scrambled egg' look to it—bits of cooked egg will be floating around in your lovely sauce! Don't despair. Cool it, then run it through a blender or food processor to remove the lumps, return it to the refrigerator, and chill it. The only effect of this second processing is that it may thin it out slightly. When you are ready to serve the eggnog, whip the cream to medium-stiff peaks. Pour the nog into a punch bowl, fold in the whipped cream so that it rises to the surface in lumps and bumps, and dust its beauty with nutmeg.

If you prefer not to use whipped cream, beat the egg whites left over from the 3 yolks, add about 50 g/2 oz of sugar to help them hold their shape, and fold them into the nog. (This produces a slightly less calorific egg nog.)

If you wish to transform this punch into a syllabub, which always has some citrus in it, all you need do is omit the vanilla and instead add a tablespoon of grated orange rind and a tablespoon of orange juice together with a teaspoon of grated lemon rind and a teaspoon of lemon juice. You can vary the amounts of orange and lemon to suit your personal preference. Nutmeg is not usually dusted over syllabub, but if you like the combination of flavours there is no reason not to add it.

Serves four

A tangy punch with lots of sparkle

Party Punch

---

1 × 190 g/7 fl oz tin frozen orange juice concentrate
150 ml/¼ pint lemon juice
3 litres/5 pints lemon- or lime-flavoured soda, such as bitter lemon
3 litres/ 5 pints pineapple juice
1 packet frozen strawberries

Add required amount of water (or soda water) to juices. Combine all of the above, putting in the soda last. If you are concerned about the punch losing its zip as the party wears on, make your ice cubes with additional soda.

Serves fifteen to twenty

These delicious after-dinner drinks are my answer to Irish Coffee:

Coffee/Chocolate

2 level teaspoons powdered instant coffee
2 heaped teaspoons cocoa
4 heaped teaspoons vanilla sugar
4 dessertspoons cold milk
350 ml/12 fl oz scalding hot milk
50 ml/2 fl oz cream, whipped

Mix the coffee, cocoa and sugar together in a small bowl. Stir in the cold milk to make a syrup. Scald the remaining milk. When ready, pour the hot milk over the syrup, beating with a whisk to blend thoroughly and create a nice froth. Pour into cups; add a dollop of whipped cream.

Additional flavourings can include vanilla essence (or substitute—see The Vanilla Dilemma), a cinnamon stick in each cup, or a dusting of cinnamon on the whipped cream.

Chocolate/Coffee

Follow the above recipe but reduce the amount of powdered instant coffee from 2 teaspoons to a half teaspoon or less. This gives you a basically chocolate-flavoured drink with just a hint of coffee to it.

If you want to make these drinks slightly less rich, either use skimmed milk or make the drink with half milk and half water.

Serves two, four in demi-tasses, or one pig.

Here's a nonalcoholic replacement for Swedish Glögg at holiday time. It can be served hot or cold, although in cold weather it's best served hot.

Spiced Grape Juice

    1 litre/1¾ pints red grape juice
    400 ml/¾ pint tea
    juice of 1 orange
    3 or 4 orange slices
    1½ tsps lemon juice
    100 g/4 oz sugar
    1 tsp cinnamon
    ¼ tsp allspice
    1 tbs Grenadine
    4 cloves (optional)

Put all the ingredients into a covered pot and bring to the boil. Reduce the heat and simmer lightly for about 5 minutes, lowering it further to warm; keep it on the stove until ready to serve. If serving cold, allow it to cool to room temperature. Run it through several layers of cheesecloth in a sieve and then bottle it in the refrigerator. You may wish to adjust the sugar up to down. As I have a distinct sweet tooth I tend to sweeten things up. If you want a sharper flavour add a few cloves.

Serves six

Before we get into desserts, I'd like to take some space here to address—

The Vanilla Dilemma: Replacing the Alcoholic Essence

When I first began entertaining recovering alcoholics, I was amazed to discover the existence of a controversy over the use of vanilla. Good heavens, I thought, vanilla? That's such innocuous stuff. Wrong, wrong, wrong. (Some of them actually drank it and exuded the aroma of vanilla from every pore for days. Apparently, in its own way, it can be as odoriferous as garlic.) I learned that recovering alcoholic friends did not even keep it in the house. How, I wondered, do you bake without vanilla? I now know that there are many ways to get vanilla flavour without using essence. My first rule is that if the alcohol in the vanilla essence is cooked to oblivion during the recipe's preparation, I sail ahead. If, however, there is the slightest chance that it will not be eliminated in the fire, I use an alternative method of separating the bad guys from the good without losing that ineffable vanilla taste. For those of you who don't want to use the essence ever, here are the alternatives I've come up with:

(Virtually all of the recipes that call for vanilla also prescribe sugar, so two of my three solutions include sugar. The third does not.)

1) Vanilla Sugar.

Put 500 g–2½ kgs/1–5 lbs of sugar (depending on how often you use it) into an airtight container with 2 vanilla beans—cut into 1"/2½ cm pieces—for each 500 g/1 lb of sugar, integrating beans and sugar to make sure the beans are evenly distributed throughout. Store at least a week (longer is better as the flavour intensifies with time).

When you use the sugar, sift it right onto your scales; return the bits of bean to the canister. This method can be used with granulated, caster, icing and brown sugar; fructose; and any granular sugar substitute.

2) *Vanilla Syrup.*

Slit open the sides of 2 to 4 beans; cut into one-inch lengths. Cover with 1 litre/1¾ pints of water. Bring to the boil and reduce by half. Let sit covered overnight. Next day, add 500 g/1 lb of sugar and bring to the boil. Cover pot for 3 minutes to steam away any crystals that might cling to the side of the pot; uncover for 3 more minutes. Allow to cool. Pour into a jar, bean bits and all, cover, and refrigerate. This will last almost indefinitely in the refrigerator. If crystals form, they can be dissolved by unscrewing the cap of the jar, placing it in a pan of hot water, and waiting a few minutes. (Be sure to let the jar come to room temperature first and to loosen the cap or it may crack.) When you use this type of vanilla, you must take the amount of sugar the recipe calls for into consideration, as more than a teaspoon can change the taste, particularly in beverages.

3) *Vanilla Cubes.*

This is the only way I've managed to make vanilla without alcohol or sugar. Start as for Vanilla Syrup except that after steeping overnight, strain the bean out, making sure to get as much pulp as possible away from the bean and into the vanilla infusion. You will wind up with vanilla-flavoured water that contains vanilla seeds. Pour this infusion into an ice cube tray—the kind that makes miniature cubes or narrow slices—and freeze. When frozen, remove from the tray and store in a freezer bag. Each cube is about a teaspoon. Unless you need a lot of vanilla, the additional liquid shouldn't affect your results.

Some recipes for custard call for the vanilla bean to be placed in the milk as it is scalded. This works, but will not give you a really good vanilla taste.

For some reason, vanilla is the only flavouring that ever comes up for discussion. Inspection of the other flavourings on my shelf reveals that orange, lemon, and almond essences are all loaded with alcohol. If you don't want to use the essence, try the infusion method, or add a bit of grated orange or lemon peel to the recipe, or some ground almonds.

While we are on the subject of flavouring, recovering alcoholics can't tell the difference between artificial flavours like rum and brandy and the real thing, and while the taste might not be totally traumatic, it will certainly startle the taster. A bit like suddenly running into an old flame who once done him or her wrong.

The Happy Ending

Ice cream bombes are often absolutely full of alcohol. This one doesn't have a drop, but does have an absolutely marvellous taste. It is the creation of Desmond Elliott.

Bombe Desmond

3 litres/5 pints rich vanilla ice cream
50 g/2 oz crystallized ginger, finely chopped
175 g/ 6 oz walnuts, finely chopped
75 g/3 oz walnuts, finely ground
50 g/2 oz honey

This recipe requires a certain amount of construction so get started on it two days or so in advance. If it has been totally prepared the day before your party, all you do on party day is unmould it, serve, and wait for the raves.

Line your mould (which can be practically anything, including an ordinary glass mixing bowl) with the ice cream and freeze for several hours or overnight (we recommend overnight). The next day, chop the walnuts, mix them with the honey, and line the ice cream layer. When the walnut/honey layer has had a chance to set—say 1 or 2 hours in the freezer—add another layer of vanilla ice cream. This second addition of ice cream needs another 4 hours or so in the freezer. Next comes a layer of chopped, crystallized ginger, and the fifth layer is the sealing layer, which is plain vanilla ice cream again. Once it's complete, it's best to leave it in the freezer again overnight. Just before serving, invert the mould and place it on a chilled (in the freezer) serving plate. Loosen the bombe by covering the mould with hot towels, remove the mould, and cover the ice cream with the ground walnuts. If for some reason you can't serve it immediately, return it to the freezer, bringing it out again about 10 or 15 minutes before serving time so that it will soften slightly.

Serves eight

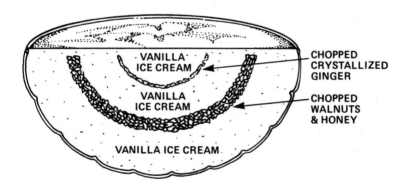

This recipe is very easy to make but you have to allow a bit of extra time for the mixture to sit as the sugar melts.

Chocolate Whipped Cream

    2 heaped teaspoons cocoa
    4 heaped teaspoons sugar
    325 ml/12 fl oz double cream
    1 teaspoon vanilla essence (or substitute—see The Vanilla Dilemma)

Mix the cocoa with the sugar, and add a few spoonfuls of double cream to moisten. As the cocoa liquefies, gradually add the rest of the cream. Cover and refrigerate for 4 to 5 hours or overnight. About 20 minutes before serving time, move it to the freezer. Put your beaters in the freezer too. When bowl and beaters emerge from the freezer, the mixture will beat up to an absolutely voluptuous cocoa whipped cream.

Makes about 700 ml/1¼ pints

Kept warm at the table, this makes a heavenly dip for fresh fruit fondue.

Fancy Chocolate Sauce

50 g/2 oz unsweetened or bitter chocolate
6 tablespoons water
100 g/4 oz sugar
pinch of salt
40g/1½ oz butter
1 tablespoon strong coffee
pinch of cinnamon

Melt the chocolate and water in a saucepan to blend. Add the sugar and salt; cook until the sugar is dissolved and the mixture is slightly thickened. Remove from heat, add the butter, strong coffee, and cinnamon. Stir to blend and return to heat just to keep warm. For an orange flavour, substitute a tablespoon of frozen orange juice concentrate for the coffee.

Makes about 225 ml/8 fl oz

A colourful one-of-a-kind dish for that special occasion when you want dessert to be memorable

Pavlova

This recipe comes from a kitchen in Christ Church, New Zealand. Pavlova, which has become much more popular here in recent years, is a marvellous dessert for a tea party or a formal dinner, and can replace such booze-laden dishes as Bavarians and mousses. The controversy between New Zealand and Australia as to which country originated Pavlova borders on outright warfare. A New Zealander will insist that it's a New Zealand recipe that was smuggled to Australia; an Australian will swear that the reverse is true. Whatever its origins, this recipe is a really good one. It is essential to follow it *exactly* if you wish to be successful. Deviations in ingredients or method can lead to a gloppy, gooey mess. And I definitely recommend that when you first try this recipe you do so on a clear, cool day—avoid a rainy day until you gain experience with rainy days and Pavlova as the extra humidity in the air can keep the meringue from developing the necessary crunchy edges.

Meringue Shell

>   3 egg whites
>   3 dessertspoons cold water
>   225 g/8 oz caster sugar
>   3 tsps cornflour
>   pinch of salt
>   ½ tsp vanilla essence (or substitute—see The Vanilla Dilemma)
>   1 tsp white distilled vinegar

Beat the egg whites until they are very stiff but not dry. Add the water one spoonful at a time and continue to beat. Add the sugar gradually, beating well. Lastly, mix in the cornflour, salt, vanilla (if you are using it), and vinegar. Pile it in the centre of an ungreased baking sheet, forming a big mound, and hollow out a crater in the centre of the mound like a volcano—make it a shallow crater with a flat bottom to it. Bake at 140°C/275°F/Gas Mark 1 for 1 hour or until it takes on a light golden colour. Turn off the oven and leave it for at least 1 hour more. Do not open the oven door after turning off the oven. If you peek, you'll disturb the baking process.

If the Pavlova has not taken on colour in the first hour of cooking, turn the heat up to 150°C/300°F/Gas Mark 2 and watch it until it does. Once you get that lovely lightly baked look, turn the oven down to 140°C/275°F/Gas Mark 1 close the door and allow the oven to reheat for 5 minutes, then turn off the oven and leave the Pavlova in it for 1 or 2 hours (no peeking!). The final texture of a proper Pavlova is crusty on the outside and soft but cooked on the inside; it's something of a cross between a giant marshmallow and an angel food cake.

The coating for the Pavlova is prepared in advance but not assembled until the interval between the main course and dessert. If you prepare this dish too far in advance, you lose the surprise of the crunch of the shell of the meringue underneath the cream coating.

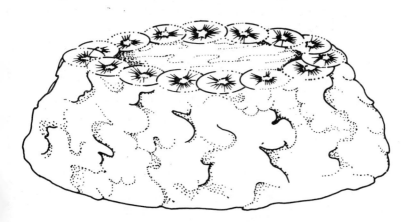

Filling and Icing:

2 kiwi fruit (if not available, use another fresh fruit that's fairly soft and slices prettily, such as peaches or nectarines.)

1 cup custard (preferably homemade although custard powder can be used.)

225 ml/8 fl oz double cream, whipped

To assemble the Pavlova: fill the volcanic crater with the custard. Whip the double cream, sweetening it slightly with plain or vanilla sugar. Cover the sides but not the top of the Pavlova with the whipped cream. Place the sliced kiwi or other fruit in a decorative pattern around the edge of the top where the custard meets the whipped cream; arrange additional fruit around the base of the Pavlova. To serve, slice with a very sharp knife that has been dipped in hot water. I wipe the knife off with a hot, damp sponge cloth in between each cut. Because it's easier to perform this surgery in the kitchen I take it to the table, let everybody gaze upon its splendour, and return to the kitchen to cut it.

There are many, many variations of Pavlova. The constants are some type of pastry cream, some type of fruit, and whipped cream. For example, you might fill the centre with a chocolate cream, use a plain white cream on the outside, and decorate with mandarin oranges. In a cold-weather version, chocolate syrup is added to the top of the cream in the centre and glacé cherries used for the decoration. Here's to cold weather!

Serves 8

This makes a very rich, soft pastry— something of a cross between biscuit and cake. Substituting ground almonds (40 g/ 1½ oz) for some of the flour in the pastry adds a nice touch.

Glazed Fruit Tart

Pastry:

      100 g/4 oz sifted flour
      50 g/2 oz sugar
      75 g/3 oz butter
      ½ tsp grated lemon rind
      1 egg yolk

Filling:

      50 g/2 oz sugar
      ¼ tsp ground allspice (or cinnamon and nutmeg mixed)
      3 large apples or peaches (or equivalent amount of pears, plums, or nectarines)

Glaze:

      40 g/1½ oz sugar
      3 tsp cornflour
      150 ml/¼ pint water
      1 tsp lemon juice
      red food colouring or a little redcurrant jelly

Sift the flour and sugar into bowl and cut butter in until it is crumbly. Stir in lemon rind and egg yolk; mix until you get a mixture that will form a ball. Press the dough against the sides and bottom of an 8″ 25 cm pie pan; don't prick it, just push it in there. Bake at 190°C/375°F/Gas Mark 5 for 10 minutes, remove and let cool; leave the oven on to bake the filling.

Mix sugar and spices in a cup; pare and slice enough fruit to make 3 layers of the fruit. Sprinkle about one third of the seasoning on each layer—about 1 tablespoon each time. Bake at 180°C/350°F/Gas Mark 4 for 40 minutes, remove from oven, and cool. (Baking time doesn't vary with the fruit; the fruits mentioned all do nicely with a 40-minute baking time.) While the tart cools, make the glaze.

Combine the cornflour with the cold water; stir until smooth and add the sugar. Bring mixture to the boil for about 3 minutes, just until it thickens. Remove from heat and add the lemon juice and either 1 drop of red food colouring or a dab of currant jelly. Pour it over the fruit. Let the tart cool for an hour or so; remove from the pan and serve. Don't refrigerate this as it can cloud the top glaze; since there is no custard in the recipe, you don't need to worry about refrigerating. Garnish with whipped cream, if you like.

Serves six to eight

A delicious way to have your apple a day.

Sparkling Apple Sorbet

175 ml/6 fl oz water
150 g/5 oz granulated sugar
375 ml/12 fl oz sparkling apple juice
½ lemon, juice and grated rind
1 egg white

Make a syrup by boiling the water and sugar together over high heat for just a few minutes, making sure that all of the granules and crystals on the sides of the pan are incorporated into the boiling liquid. Put the syrup into a bowl and allow it to cool. Pour the sparkling apple juice over the syrup and stir briefly with a spatula. Add the lemon juice and the grated, coloured part of the lemon rind. Beat the egg white with a whisk or fork just until it becomes foamy and add it to the mixture. Stir well; transfer to any standard ice cream maker and freeze according to its instructions.

Serves 4

I like this recipe far better than any of the ones made with alcohol. Lemon or orange essences (or substitutes) can be used in place of vanilla, depending on what you plan to serve the sauce with. A bit of freshly grated nutmeg can also add a distinctive flavour.

---

* Hard Sauce

This recipe can easily be increased, but the basic proportions are:

> 100 g/4 oz sifted icing sugar
> 100 g/4 oz butter
> ½ tsp vanilla essence (or substitute—see The Vanilla Dilemma)
> milk or cream as needed

The trick with good hard sauce is to get the texture as light as you can before the butter begins to separate. In order to do this it's best to start with butter that's soft enough to work but hard enough to hold itself together (not so soft that it's starting to sit down in the dish).

Using an electric beater, begin by creaming the butter and gradually adding the sugar. Note the texture as you proceed. If you are using the liquid vanilla syrup or the frozen vanilla cubes, add gradually at this time and continue to observe the texture. If it seems too stiff (it should just hold peaks when you raise the beater), add milk or cream as you continue to beat—just until you reach the point when the texture starts to change. Look for just the

---

Editor's Note: Hard sauce is the American version of what we call Brandy Butter. It would clearly be a bad idea to call it 'Brandy' Butter in this particular book so the American name has been left.

faintest hint of a slight separation of the butter. At this point stop beating immediately and use a scraper to clean the beaters and the bowl. Put the hard sauce into a decorative dish, cover it, and refrigerate. This holds for days and days and can be prepared well ahead of time for use during the big holidays. Remove from the refrigerator about a half-hour before serving so that it's cool but not hard and cold.

Makes 225 g/8 oz

This variation of nonalcoholic hard sauce is excellent over hot mince pie or bread pudding.

Hot Hard Sauce, Wild Variation

50 g/2 oz sifted icing sugar (see The Vanilla Dilemma)
100 g/4 oz butter
175 ml/6 fl oz double cream, whipped

Beat the butter into the sifted icing sugar. Fold in the whipped cream. (You can prepare it to this stage ahead of time.) Just before serving, heat the sauce in a saucepan and boil until it starts to foam. Put it into a heated sauce boat, serve immediately, and watch your guests gobble it up.

Makes about 450 ml/¾ pint

This is terrific with plum pudding

Foamy Sauce

100 g/4 oz butter
100 g/4 oz icing sugar
1 egg
2 tbs hot water
1 tsp vanilla essence (or substitute—see the Vanilla Dilemma)

Cream butter and gradually add sugar, egg, and hot water. Place mixture in a double boiler over hot water—at the barely bubbling stage—and continue to beat until it thickens. When thickened, remove from heat and add vanilla; beat until it is combined.

Makes about 600 ml/1 pint

This is an old American favourite which is an excellent substitute for things like plum pudding, which can be quite difficult to make at home. Although it is very easy to make, it does take a bit of time.

Indian Pudding

150 g/5 oz yellow corn meal★
1 litre/1¾ pints milk
50 g/2 oz butter
75 g/3 oz molasses or black treacle
1 tsp salt
50 g/2 oz brown sugar, tightly packed
1½ tsp cinnamon

Scald all but 300 ml/½ pint of the milk in the top of a double boiler (or in a small pot that will fit over another pot to make a makeshift double boiler). Meanwhile, mix the corn meal with the remaining cold milk. Add the cold corn meal/milk mixture to the scalding milk, stirring constantly. Place it over boiling water and cook for about 20 to 30 minutes, stirring frequently. Add the butter, molasses, salt, sugar, and cinnamon and pour into a greased baking dish, 5″ × 9″ × 3″/13 cm × 23 cm × 7½ cm deep. Bake at 160°/325°F/Gas Mark 3 for 2 hours and 15 minutes, remove from the oven, and allow to cool slightly. This dish is traditionally served warm, with either whipped cream or vanilla ice cream, and/or hard sauce for those who have a very sweet tooth.

Serves six

★ Now widely available in this country.

An optional 75 g/3 oz of toasted almonds added to the filling can give a lovely crunchiness to:

Old-Fashioned Butterscotch Pie

1 baked 9-inch/23 cm pie case
100 g/4 oz light brown sugar
50 g/2 oz dark brown sugar
45 g/1½ oz flour
¼ tsp salt
450 ml/¾ pint milk
3 egg yolks
15 g/½ oz butter
1 tsp vanilla essence (or substitute—see The Vanilla Dilemma)

Mix the sugars, flour, and salt; add milk and egg yolks and mix well. Cover and cook over low heat until thickened. Stir in butter and vanilla. Place in pie case, top with meringue, and bake at 180°C/350°F/Gas Mark 4 for 12 to 15 minutes.

Meringue:

3 egg whites
⅛ tsp salt
75 g/3 oz caster sugar

Beat the egg whites until frothy. Slowly add the sugar, beating until stiff.

Serves eight

We've nicknamed this 'virgin' trifle as on several occasions we're served this and the traditional spiritous version at the same meal.

English Trifle

48 prepared sponge fingers (or trifle sponges or slightly stale swiss roll or a combination of these)
125–175 ml/4–6 fl oz strong orange juice
1 tsp lemon juice
175 g/6 oz strawberry, raspberry, or other red jam
65 g/2½ oz blanched whole almonds
3 pears, peaches, nectarines or similar fruit, sliced
450 ml/¾ pint prepared vanilla custard
225 ml/8 fl oz whipping cream
2 tsps vanilla sugar
glacé cherries, angelica for decoration

Line the bottom of an attractive glass dish with the cake in a decorative pattern. Add the lemon juice to the orange juice and sprinkle it over the stale cake. Shake it liberally all over the cake but don't get it so wet that it's absolutely soaked. The staler the cake the more you need to use to soften it. (The original purpose of adding liquid to the sponge fingers was to return freshness to cake that had seen better days.) The next layer consists of a red jam or jelly, like strawberry or raspberry jam or redcurrant jelly. Spread this generously over the cake and add the almonds. The sliced fruit comes next: pears, peaches, apricots, nectarines—anything you choose. A layer of custard then covers the fruit. This can be made from scratch, but custard powder may be used, although not nearly as good. The hot custard is poured over the fruit and should nearly fill the bowl. If you are making a really big trifle and you need more than 450 ml/¾ pint, make extra custard. The trifle then goes into the refrigerator to chill until nearly serving time, to be finished just before the meal or between the main course and dessert. For the finale you'll need whipping cream that's very, very cold; whip it, adding vanilla sugar as you go until it is slightly sweetened. Then, depending on your decorative skills (and how much time you have) you can be fancy and use a pastry bag with a fluted tip to pipe rosettes all over the surface of your trifle. Top each of the rosettes with a red cherry, adding pieces of green angelica on either side to make leaves. Or you can mound the whipped cream in the centre, or cover the whole surface with whipped cream, swirling it as you go, and adding cherries and angelica around the edge to form a circular pattern.

Trifle lends itself beautifully to a wide range of variations as the dessert was created originally to make use of leftovers. It remains an admirable dish for that very purpose.

Serves eight

A traditional dessert that always seems to appear on a restaurant trolley is Pears Poached in Red Wine. While the poaching does remove the alcohol from the wine, the surviving wine 'remembrance' may be traumatic to the palates of guests who are recovering alcoholics. This recipe for pears poached in either red or white grape juice (depending on the colour desired) fits the bill without bringing back the unhappy memories.

Pears Poached in Grape Juice

6 to 8 firm pears
700–900 ml/1¼–1½ pints grape juice
100 g/4 oz sugar
1 stick cinnamon
3 cloves

Pour the juice into a pot, add the sugar, stick of cinnamon, and cloves. Bring to the boil and set aside to cool. In the meantime, peel the pears, if necessary cutting off a slice on the bottom so that they will stand up straight, but leave the stem on top of the pear (they look much prettier when they have a stem showing). Gently lower the pears into the liquid and return the pan to the heat, making sure the liquid covers the pears. They don't have to be sitting upright for this process; they can lean a bit as long as they are under the liquid. Bring the liquid to simmering point—it's important not to boil it at this point as you may break up the pears. The pears you use for this particular recipe should not be terribly ripe or they won't make it through the cooking process.

Simmer the pears for 20 to 25 minutes or until they are cooked through. Stand the pears up on their bottoms so that they have a resting place. If you allow them to cool on their sides they'll have a dent on their hips (and who needs dented hips?). Cover the pan and set the pears aside to cool in the poaching liquid. Before serving, remove the pears from the poaching liquid, seat them on a platter, remove the cinnamon and cloves from the poaching liquid, return it to the stove, and boil it down rapidly. When the poaching liquid is reduced to approximately 150 ml/¼ pint remove it from the heat and stir it to speed the cooling process. Either pour it on the platter under the pears and set the pears in it, or pour it over the pears. If you have poached your pears in white grape juice, serve them on vanilla ice cream with hot fudge sauce and voilà! You have the classic Poires Belle Hélène.

Serves six to eight

Sugar 'n' spice 'n' other things nice

Cinnamon Poached Pears

6 underripe pears
900 ml/1½ pints water
400 g/14 oz sugar
1 tbs lemon juice
1 tsp grated lemon rind
2 cinnamon sticks
4 whole cloves

Peel the pears and drop them into lemon water to keep them from turning brown. In a large pot bring water, sugar, lemon juice and rind to the boil, add the cinnamon stick, cloves, and pears. Cover and keep the syrup at a rolling boil for 5 minutes. Simmer the pears 20 to 25 minutes, or until they are fork tender; move them to a flat-bottomed dish to cool. Stand them up, pour some of the syrup over them, and chill. Serve this with the following creamy sauce:

Custard Sauce

225 ml/8 fl oz milk
150 ml/¼ pint double cream
2½ cm/1″ piece of vanilla bean
75 g/3 oz sugar

4 large egg yolks
2 tsps cornflour

Combine the milk and cream, add the piece of vanilla bean, and bring the mixture to scalding. Meanwhile, beat the egg yolks in a separate bowl, adding the sugar and beating until light and lemon-coloured. Dissolve the cornflour in a little of the cold milk and set aside. Remove the vanilla bean from the scalded milk and, off the heat, pour a little of the scalded milk into the cornflour mixture, returning the mixture to the main pot. Put pot back over heat, bring it to the boil, allowing the cornflour to thicken it slightly. Take the thickened milk off the heat and pour it in a steady stream over the egg yolks while beating constantly. Return the mixture to the saucepan and return to the heat, stirring constantly as you bring it just to the boil. You must not boil this mixture as the egg yolks would separate, but you do bring it right *up to* that point. You'll notice that the egg yolks will thicken it a bit more. Take off the heat, stir occasionally to let the steam out and to prevent a skin from forming, and cool.

Serves six

Glazed and gorgeous.

Sautéed Pears with Walnuts

6 firm pears, peeled and sliced (use the ones with the
brown skins, if you can get them, otherwise any
firm pear will do)
50 g/ 2 oz unsalted butter
75 ml/2 fl oz lemon juice
65 g/2½ oz dark brown sugar
175 g/6 oz chopped walnuts
150 ml/¼ pint apple juice

In a large frying pan, sauté half the pears and 25 g/1 oz of
the butter over high heat, shaking the pan for 3 to 5
minutes or until they are just tender. Transfer them to a
serving platter. Sauté the remaining pears in the remaining butter in the same manner. Add to the pan the lemon
juice, sugar, walnuts, and apple juice. Cook the mixture
over moderately high heat, swirling the frying pan until
the mixture is reduced to a thick glaze. Drizzle the glaze
over the pears and serve with whipped cream.

Serves six

These especially rich biscuits are wonderful at tea. Because they are incredibly light and delicate, they must be assembled at the very last minute or they turn soggy. You do need one special piece of equipment to make these: the textured rolling pin with points on it that gives this biscuit its name.

Parisian Waffles

Biscuits:

> 225 g/8 oz butter
> 175 g/6 oz flour (plus an additional 25 g/1 oz if necessary)
> ¾ dessertspoon whipping cream

Filling:

> 1 egg yolk
> 25 g/1 oz soft butter
> 1 tablespoon cream
> 175 g/6 oz icing sugar (approximately)

Cut the butter and flour together, adding just enough cream to moisten the mixture and allow it to form a ball, which you refrigerate for at least 1 hour. (My experience has been that chilling it for an afternoon produces better results.) Roll it out (with a regular rolling pin) until it's about ³/8″/1 cm thick, then roll once again with the textured rolling pin to produce the waffle structure. Cut the biscuits into squares (or oblongs or diamonds) and sprinkle lightly with granulated sugar. Separate and place on an ungreased baking sheet. Bake at 190°C/375°F/Gas Mark 5 for 10 minutes, at which point you will discover whether you have added enough flour. This biscuit is somewhat tricky in that on certain days you may need to add the extra flour and on certain days you may not.

When in doubt, add the extra flour as it won't destroy the texture of the biscuit. While the biscuits are baking, prepare the filling.

Beat the butter until fluffy. Add the egg yolk, icing sugar, and carefully, drop by drop, add the cream until it reaches a nice spreading consistency—like cake icing.

At the last minute, and only after the biscuits are thoroughly cool, ice the flat side of half of them generously with the filling and top them with the rest to make sandwiches.

Makes about 2 dozen

These delightful little cakes often show up soused with booze at tea parties or after dinner, ruined for many dessert lovers either by being drenched in some kind of alcohol or wearing an icing or filling that is similarly laced with spirits. This usually quite complicated recipe is simplified here for pretty petits fours at home. Nevertheless, it's best to prepare the cake two days ahead of time and the petits fours a day ahead as their preparation does require your undivided attention.

Petits Fours

Cake:

> 275 g/10 oz sifted plain flour
> 250 g/9 oz vanilla sugar (see the Vanilla Dilemma)
> 3 tsp baking powder
> 1 teaspoon salt (optional)
> 2 eggs, separated
> 75 ml/⅛ pint oil, preferably tasteless
> 225 ml/8 fl oz milk

Grease a swiss roll pan and line the bottom with wax or parchment paper. Grease the paper and sprinkle it with plain bread crumbs, tilting the pan until it is evenly covered; shake out any excess. Sift the flour, 225 g/8 oz sugar, baking powder, and salt together several times to be sure that these ingredients are well combined. In a large, excruciatingly clean bowl, using squeaky-clean beaters, beat the egg whites until they are foamy and hold soft peaks. Sprinkle in remainder of the sugar, little by little, beating continuously until the meringue forms the soft peaks again. Stir the oil and half of the milk into the flour mixture; beat for several minutes with an electric mixer. Stir in the beaten egg yolks, the remaining milk,

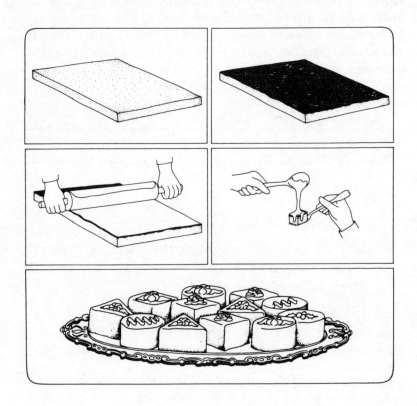

and vanilla, and beat another minute. Carefully fold in the meringue until it has been completely incorporated. Pour mixture into the prepared pan. Bake at 180°C/ 350°F/Gas Mark 4 for 30 minutes or until the top of the cake springs back when touched lightly. Cool in the pan for a few minutes—until the cake stops steaming—and run a knife around the edges; turn the pan over onto a large cake rack or clean dishtowel. Carefully peel off the wax paper, put the cake on a rack (you may have to put two together), and cool completely. Wrap the cake tightly in wax paper covered with aluminium foil and store in a cool place overnight.

Next day, when you are ready to begin the icing and decorating process, cover a counter in the kitchen with aluminium foil or wax paper and set up your cake racks. You are about to make one of the world's most glorious messes!

Unwrap the cake and cut off the side crusts. The next few steps will vary, depending on the kind of taste you want. I personally like the flavour of almond and raspberry, but many people prefer apricot. You will need:

1 jar of your favourite kind of seedless jam
100 g/4 oz sugar
225 ml/8 fl oz water
225 g/8 oz prepared marzipan
2 tablespoons spreadable honey (optional)

Roll the marzipan out until it is the same shape as the cake (with its crusts removed) before it has been cut. Spread a little honey or some of the jam across the top of the cake, just enough to hold the marzipan in place, gently lower the marzipan onto the cake, and pat it down all around. Then cut the cake.

You may cut your cake into a number of different shapes or you may cut the whole thing into a single shape. I usually make a combination of squares and diamonds, cutting half of the cake into squares or oblongs and the other half into diamonds. If you want to be really fancy you can take deep pastry cutters and cut other shapes as well.

Heat the sugar and water in a saucepan, stirring to dissolve all the sugar crystals, and boil without stirring until it reaches 230°C on a sugar thermometer. Remove from heat and stir in the whole jar of jam. Holding the little cakes one at a time on a fork over the saucepan, spoon the sugar/jam glaze over them and then put aside on the wire rack.

The little cakes with the sticky jam coating will need to dry for several hours or until they are firm but still sticky. (Don't worry about going away and leaving them for quite a while; they'll always be sticky, like certain romances.) The final layer can either be a butter-cream icing (a little tricky as you have to actually spread it) or a fondant icing, which is a bit more trouble to prepare but far easier to put on because you can drip it over the cakes. If you choose the butter-cream icing, use our recipe for hard sauce—simply thin it out with enough cream to make it easy to spread. Here is the recipe for the more classic fondant icing:

Fondant Icing

> 500 g/1¼ lb granulated sugar
> ¼ tsp cream of tartar PLUS one extra pinch
> 500 ml/18 fl oz water
> 750 g/1½ lbs icing sugar (prepared as vanilla sugar)
> 1½ tsps lemon juice
> Yellow food colouring
> Pink food colouring
> Orange food colouring

Combine the granulated sugar, cream of tartar, and water in a large saucepan. Stir carefully over low heat to dissolve all of the sugar crystals; then cook without stirring to 226°C on a sugar thermometer. Remove from heat, set aside, and cool down to 125°C. Don't rush this stage; it won't work if you do. Gradually beat the vanilla icing sugar and salt into the boiled mixture until it is a smooth, thick syrup. It will take all of the sugar given in the recipe and perhaps a little more to give it the right texture. It's impossible to give you a precise measurement because a lot will depend on the weather. Take some of the mixture and put it in a bowl. Holding each little cake over the bowl with a fork, spoon a layer of icing over the top to cover it and put it back on the rack to dry. You will notice that the glaze, particularly if you have used a red raspberry glaze, still shows through. Don't worry, as you will be putting a second coating of fondant on the cakes. Again let the cakes stand for a few hours or until the icing has set.

When it's time to add the next coat, divide the remaining icing (carefully scraping up any drips from underneath the cake rack so that they can be remelted and used again) into 4 bowls. Stir a little bit of pink food colouring into one bowl, a little bit of the orange into another and the lemon juice and a little bit of yellow into the third, just to get the merest pastel tint. Leave the fourth one to make some of your petits fours white. Drip the coloured frostings over the cakes. If the fondant is getting a little too thick to handle (you want it reasonably thick for coverage, but you also want it to pour), put in a tiny bit of hot water and it will thin right down. Really put this in by the drop or you may end up with a soupy mess, although if you make this mistake, a little added icing sugar should get you out of trouble.

Decorating the top of the cakes is usually done with butter icing. Use our recipe for hard sauce, but hold back a little bit of the cream so that you have a slightly stiffer icing. This can be divided into batches tinted slightly different colours. You can make a simple and pretty decoration by using a star tip on your pastry bag to create rosettes in various colours on the cakes, adding leaves by using a leaf tip and tinting some of the icing green. Once iced, these little cakes store nicely overnight for your party the following day. If they are kept in a single layer, tightly tinned, they will hold for the better part of a week, although I prefer to let them do their thing as early as possible. When they do, your guests are sure to be pleased by your painstaking efforts on their behalf. Your creations will both look and taste scrumptious.

Makes about 5 to 6 dozen petit fours

Plum Pudding

As it is virtually impossible to buy ready-made plum puddings which contain no alcohol you must make your own. Do not fear that the lack of beer or stout will make for a pale pudding. As long as it is made far enough before Christmas it will be as dark as usual. Simply substitute milk for the beer and omit the brandy or rum.

I don't wish to appear immodest, but this truly is:

The World's Best Fudge Sauce

150 g/5 oz unsweetened chocolate* (or plain)
150 ml/¼ pint milk
150 ml/¼ pint double cream
¼ tsp salt (optional)
1 tbs golden syrup
175 g/6 oz sugar
¼ to 1 tsp instant coffee or other flavouring—see below
25 g/1 oz butter or margarine

Heat chocolate, sugar, milk, cream, syrup, and salt in a saucepan, stirring until the chocolate is melted and the mixture is smooth. Bring to the boil, stirring constantly, and cook 2 to 4 minutes or just until the sugar is completely dissolved. (NOTE: Be careful not to boil it too long or you'll end up with fudge instead of sauce.) Remove from heat, stir in butter and, if desired, add instant coffee or other flavouring. Serve warm or store in refrigerator. It will solidify as it gets cold but can easily be reheated over hot water.

If you leave out the coffee, the sauce will have a pure chocolate taste rather than a chocolate/coffee taste. You can also add a teaspoon of frozen concentrated orange juice at the end to make it chocolate/orange, or cherry juice to make it chocolate/cherry. In winter you might like a touch of cinnamon, but use a light hand as a little goes a long way.

* Baker's unsweetened chocolate is available in some upmarket stores here & does make a better sauce. However a good plain chocolate may be substituted

This basic chocolate sauce can be used over pastry or ice cream or thinned down with additional milk and used as a base for chocolate milk or shakes. If you do plan to use it for beverage, it's best to use a blender as this sauce will not disperse in the liquid as easily as a cocoa-based syrup.

Makes about 600 ml/1 pint

A redefinition of the traditionally Curacao and Kirsch-laden dessert. The crêpe recipe for this dish appears in 'Assorted Specialities'. The crêpes can be prepared ahead and stored in the refrigerator; put pieces of wax paper between them and closely cover with plastic wrap.

Crêpes Suzette

1 tbs orange rind, just the coloured part, finely grated

1½ tsps lemon rind, finely grated

80 ml/3 fl oz Grenadine

80 ml/3 fl oz frozen orange concentrate

30 ml/1 fl oz sour cherry Nectar (*Lindavia* make a good one)

1 teaspoon strong vanilla sugar (see The Vanilla Dilemma)

100 g/4 oz unsalted butter, melted in a fairly large frying pan (big enough so that you can arrange 8 of the pancakes in it).

When the butter begins to bubble, add the lemon rind, orange rind, and sugar. Then add the Grenadine, frozen orange concentrate, and sour cherry juice. Cook and stir, allowing the sauce to bubble until it cooks down a bit and begins to thicken. Take the pan off the heat and dip each crêpe into the sauce until thoroughly coated and hot (this takes a very short time per crêpe), fold it into quarters, and put it off to the side of the pan. Just before serving sprinkle a little granulated sugar across the top of each crêpe; serve very hot.

You will want to taste this recipe for sweetness to make sure it's at the level that you personally prefer. If you like it a bit sweeter after you try it the first time, add a bit more sugar in the beginning.

Serves eight

*The traditional recipe for Zabaglione uses Marsala and the
many variations use Grand Marnier, Curacao, or Cointreau.
My version, which uses none of the above, has stood up very
well to taste tests.*

Zabaglione

3 egg yolks
100 g/4 oz sugar
60 ml/2 fl oz frozen orange concentrate
1 tsp lemon juice

Put all of the ingredients in the top of a double boiler and
beat for a minute with a portable electric mixer until they
are combined. Place over boiling water, beating constantly, until the mixture becomes foamy and holds soft
peaks, like whipped cream. This dessert can be served
immediately just the way it is. Put it in a wine or
champagne glass and sprinkle a little granulated sugar
mixed with grated lemon and orange peel over the top of
each glass.

If you want to use it as a sauce for cold fruit or for fruit
and ice cream, remove it from the heat as soon as it is
cooked and set the double boiler in a basin of cold water
with a few ice cubes floating around in it. Continue to
beat the Zabaglione until cool. It will lose quite a bit of its
volume but will retain the texture and its peaks. Separately,
whip 225 ml/8 fl oz of double cream, fold the cooled
Zabaglione into the double cream, and refrigerate. This
sauce can be held for several hours. With layers of fresh
fruit and ice cream it makes a lovely Zabaglione parfait.
Zabaglione is especially good over strawberries or
peaches, hot or cold.

Serves four

Butterscotch Date Brownies

50 g/2 oz butter, melted
225 g/8 oz dark brown sugar
1 egg
¼ tsp salt
75 g/3 oz plain flour
1 tsp baking powder
½ tsp vanilla essence (or substitute—see The Vanilla Dilemma)
75 g/3 oz walnuts, broken in pieces
75 g/3 oz dates, stoned and chopped roughly.

Mix all ingredients together thoroughly and put in well-greased, shallow 8″ × 8″ pan. Bake in preheated 180°C/350°F/Gas Mark 4 oven. Cut in squares while still warm.

Serves 16 or more

Midnight Cake

100 g/4 oz refined vegetable fat such as Trex or
Cookeen
275 g/10 oz sugar
2 eggs
225 ml/8 fl oz hot water
50 g/2 oz cocoa
175 g/6 oz sifted plain flour
½ tsp salt
½ tsp bicarbonate of soda
1 tsp baking powder
1 tsp vanilla essence (or substitute—see The Vanilla
Dilemma)

Cream the fat, gradually add the sugar, and cream until
fluffy. Blend in the well-beaten eggs. In a separate container, slowly add hot water to the cocoa; mix carefully
until completely smooth. Sift flour, salt, bicarb, and baking powder together and gradually add to the creamed
mixture, alternating with the cocoa mixture. Add vanilla
essence or substitute. Pour either into an 8″ square pan
that's 2½″ deep or into two 8″ round pans.★ Bake at
180°C/350°F/Gas Mark 4 for 50 to 55 minutes for the
square pan or about 35 minutes for the round pans. The
cake is done when it just barely springs back when
touched in the centre. This cake is the basis for my triple
chocolate cake, which drives chocolate lovers wild.

Serves six to eight

★   If you've ever done battle with a layer of cake that didn't slide
smoothly from the pan, you're a likely candidate for trying my
sure-fire method: Cut a piece of wax paper to exactly fit the pan, put
it in the greased pan, then grease *over* the wax paper and sprinkle
plain bread crumbs on it, tilting the pan so that the entire bottom is

Chocoholics on your guest list? Give them a triple treat with his gloriously rich dessert.

Triple Chocolate Cake

3 layers Midnight Cake
1 double recipe Chocolate Fudge (dark) Icing
1 double recipe Cocoa or French Cream (light) Icing
100 g/4 oz seedless raspberry jam, melted

Brush crumbs from the cake. Frost the bottom layer with light chocolate icing and spread with melted raspberry jam. Top with the dark chocolate icing. Add the next layer and repeat the process. Add top layer and ice it with the raspberry jam only. Ice the top and sides with the remaining light icing. Use the dark icing to decorate the top and sides.

Serves eight to ten

covered (not the sides, which will have just the grease). When the cake is done, let it rest in the pan for 5 or 6 minutes or until it's not steaming hot. Loosen around the edges with a knife, put a cake rack over the top of the pan, and turn it upside down. Put the cake rack down on the counter and gently lift the cake pan off the cake. Carefully peel away the wax paper with a blunt knife. Your cake will have a perfect surface every time. You can also do this with troublesome brownies and flapjacks when it's important that they look 'just so' at serving time.

Hardly a calorie in a carload . . .

Dark Chocolate Icing For Triple Chocolate Cake

75 g/3 oz butter
⅛ tsp salt
450 g/1 lb icing sugar (treated for vanilla flavour)
100 g/4 oz unsweetened or plain chocolate, melted and cooled
2 or 3 tablespoons milk or cream

Cream the butter, add the salt, and gradually add the sugar. As you continue to beat, add a little bit of the milk or cream, keeping the mixture at a manageable consistency. Add the melted and cooled chocolate and as much milk as necessary to give the icing a good spreading consistency.

Ices top and sides of standard 2-layer cake

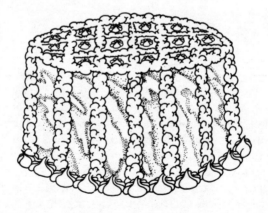

This light chocolate icing, delightful in and of itself, makes a wonderful second level beneath the dark icing of the triple chocolate cake. Its one drawback is that because it contains an egg, it must be refrigerated after it has been prepared. This means that you must refrigerate the whole cake, which is not the case when you use the light cocoa icing, because it contains no egg. Depending on how much storage space you have, you may prefer to stick with the cocoa icing.

French Cream Chocolate Icing

175 g/6 oz butter
450 g/1 lb icing sugar
1 egg
150 g/5 oz unsweetened or plain chocolate, melted and cooled
1 tsp vanilla essence (or substitute—see The Vanilla Dilemma)

Cream the butter until soft but not oily, and gradually add the sugar, beating all the while. Add the egg, beat in thoroughly, and blend in the chocolate and vanilla. Beat until the icing reaches spreading consistency, thinning with a little milk if necessary.

Ices top and sides of standard 2-layer cake

This is one of the possibilities for the light frosting on the triple chocolate cake. I like this one because it looks so much like those marvellous confections you see in bakeries and fancy restaurants; you know, the ones that invariably have some demon rum tucked away among the calories.

Cocoa Frosting

> 25 g/8 oz sifted vanilla-flavoured icing sugar (see The Vanilla Dilemma)
> $\frac{1}{8}$ tsp salt (this time it's not optional—the icing won't taste right without this small addition of salt)
> 15g /½ oz cocoa
> 75 g/1½ oz butter
> 3 dessertspoons hot milk
> ½ tsp vanilla syrup (also described in The Vanilla Dilemma)

Sift the sugar, salt, and cocoa together. Cream the butter until it is soft but will stand up. Add a little bit of the sugar mixture gradually, beating thoroughly. Gradually add the remaining sugar, alternating with the hot milk; beat well after each addition. Depending on the weather you may need to hold back a little milk or to add a bit more for the right result, which spreads easily but will hold its shape in peaks.

Ices top and sides of standard 2-layer cake

Appendix

Names and addresses of distributors of non-alcoholic wines and beers:

In Great Britain:

Leisure Drinks Limited
24 Willow Road
Trent Lane
Castle Donington
Derby DE7 2NP

Frank Wright Monday
Yanworth House
Yanworth
Cheltenham
Gloucestershire

Old Norfolk Punch
Welle Manor Hall
Upwell
Norfolk

In Australia:

For the Robinvale wines:

G. Caracatsanoudis & Sons
Robinvale, Victoria

For the Kaiser Stuhl wines:

Kaiser Stuhl
Sturt Highway, Nuriootpa
South Australia

For the Chateau Yaldara wines:

Chateau Yaldara
Lyndoch, South Australia

For the San Bernadino wines:

San Bernadino Winery
Griffith, New South Wales

For the Malva wines:

Malva Drink Company
684 Albany Highway,
East Victoria Park
West Australia

For the Castella wines:

Billabong Wines
Griffith
New South Wales

John Anderson and Neil Shepherd of:

Fox Valley Store
126 Fox Valley Road,
Wahroonga
New South Wales
Supply customers throughout Australia with de-alcoholized wines.

Robert Cooper of:

Caselot Drinks,
1681 Pacific Highway,
Wahroonga
New South Wales.

Index

A

Airline travel, drinking and, 31, 82
Alcohol
  accidental serving of, 19
  flavours, artificial, 45
  hidden in beverages, 60
Alcoholic, drinking, 24, 89
Alcoholic, recovering, 15
  accidental serving of alcohol, 19
  dining in restaurants, 90, 92–95
  party ideas from, 26–30
  returning to entertaining, 27
  The Slip, how to handle, 66
  and wine sauces, 64
Alcoholism
  characteristic symptoms of the
      disease, 12
  as a disease, 12
  physical aspects of, 24
  recovery from, 13
Allergy
  to alcohol, 24
  to food, 24
Almond essence, substitutions for,
  46
Anger, in drinking guest, 24
Apéritifs, alcohol-free, 37
Apple Juice, Mulled, 181
Apple sorbet, sparkling, 199
August Bank holiday party, 102
Australia, non-drinker's favourites
  in, 37–39

B

Babysitter service, providing for
    guests, 62
Bacon, noodle casserole, 157
Bar
  dry, 23, 53, 69, 73
  wet, 23, 53, 69, 72
Bars, wine, 79
Beef
  braised in beer, 148
  burgundy, 145
  marinade for, 164
  meatloaf, 150
  stock, quick, 124
Beer, nonalcoholic
  alcohol content of, 22
Beverages
  blender drinks for recovering
      alcoholics, 42
  champagne cocktail, 179
  chocolate/coffee, 185
  Christmas fruit punch, 180
  coffee/chocolate, 185
  disadvantages of similar colours
      of alcoholic and
      nonalcoholic, 61
  dry, 33–35
  eggnog, nonalcoholic, 182
  for Brunch, 60, 61
  glasses for alcoholic, 54, 69
  glasses for nonalcoholic, 54, 69
  mulled apple juice, 181

party punch, 184
punch, 69
slightly wet, 36–38
spiced grape juice, 186
Syllabub, nonalcoholic, 182
Blender, separate for dry bar, 53
Blue cheese salad dressing, 169
Braising liquid
for meat, 50
for poultry, 50
Brandy, substitutions for, 48
Breakfast, 62, 86
appropriate time for, 62
menu, 108
order of service, 62
in a restaurant, 95
Brownies, Butterscotch, 225
Brunch,
beverages for, 60
champagne, 60
menus, 109, 110
order of service, 61
Buffets,
how to handle latecomers, 63
order of service, 66
Business events,
breakfast, 78
combining with pleasure, 77
dinner, 88
management seminar, 91
meeting with caterer, 90
nonfood, 80
overnight event, 84–89
power lunch, 79
sales conference, 91
tea, 60
Butterscotch Brownies, 225
Butterscotch pie, old fashioned, 205

C

Cake
midnight, 226
petit fours, 215–220
triple chocolate, construction of,
227
Calvados, substitutions for, 48, 51
Carbonnades à la Flamande;
see Braised beef in beer

Carrot soup, 118
Carrots
for beef burgundy, 145
puréed, 119
Cassis, substitutions for, 48
Casserole, bacon, noodle
cheese and tomato, 157
Caterers, planning, nonalcoholic
and mixed events, 90
Cauliflower soup, 119
Champagne cocktail, almost
nonalcoholic, 179
Cheese
fondue, 158
roquefort almond balls, 156
Chicken breasts
in cream sauce, 137
plain poached, 143
livers, devilled, 140
liver paté, 155
Chicken, stewed; see coq au no vin,
135
Chicken stock, quick, 125
Chicken, vol-au-vent, 141
Chocolate icing
cocoa, 230
dark, 228
French cream, 229
Chocolate cake
midnight, 226
Triple, 227
Chocolate sauce
Fancy, 193
fudge, 221
Chocolate whipped cream, 192
Chocolate coffee beverage, 185
Christmas punch, 180
Christmas Day Dinner, 104
Christmas Eve, white dinner, 104
Cider, substitutions for, 48
Cocktail party,
invitation for, 54
new do's and don'ts, 52
Cocktail, champagne, 179
Coffee,
correct technique for making, 40,
41
dark roasts, 40
Irish, nonalcoholic answer to, 185

light roasts, 40
proper storage of beans and
    ground coffee, 41
Coffee/chocolate, hot
    beverage, 185
Cognac,
    substitutions for, 45
Cointreau,
    substitutions for, 46
Coq au no vin, chicken, 135
Coquilles St. Jacques, 126
Cream of tomato soup, 121
Cream tea
    menu, 58, 59
Cream soda, in Trifle, 46
Crêpes Suzette, 223
Crêpes, asparagus and cheese, 162
Crêpes
    savoury, 162
    sweet, 162
Cucumber mousse, 154
Curacao, substitutions for, 46
Curry
    Lady Curzon soup, 123
    sauce, cold for fish or fruit, 163
    soup, carrot, 119
    soup, cauliflower, 120
Custard, 210

D

Dark rum, substitutions for, 45
Day At The Races Picnic, 101
Dessert
    apple sorbet, sparkling, 199
    crêpes Suzette, 223
    glazed fruit tart, 197
    ice cream, Bombe Desmond, 190
    Indian pudding, 204
    Pavlova, 194
    pears, sautéed with walnuts, 212
    pears, poached in cinnamon, 210
    pears, poached in grape juice, 208
    plum pudding, 220
    trifle, English, 206
    zabaglione, 224
Dijon mustard
    prepared without wine, 51

as substitute for cognac, 51
Dinner
    business, 88
    invitation to, 63
    late, pre-ordering food and drink,
        91
    menus, 113–114
    in a restaurant, 92
    seating latecomers, 63
Drinking guest
    and driving, 25
    how to handle drunkenness, 25
    personality change in, 24
Driver the, abstaining for the
        occasion, 22
Drunk driving laws, 17
    in Scandinavia, 22
Dry bar; see Bar
Duck, marinade for, 165

E

Easter Dinner, 100
Egg crêpes, 161
    fillings for, 162
Eggnog, nonalcoholic, 182
Event, seated, 23

F

Fish, poaching liquid for, 49
Fillets, poached, 134
Fitness, physical, 17
Flavouring
    almond, 46
    artificial alcohol, 72
    brandy, 45
    Calvados, 48, 51
    Cassis, 48
    cider, substitutions for, 48
    cognac, 45
    lemon, 46
    orange, 46
    raspberry, 44
    rum, 45
    sherry, 47
    vanilla, 187–189
Foamy sauce, 203

Fondue, cheese, 158
Food, with alcohol, labels for, 71, 74
Framboise, substitutions for, 44
Fruit
  cup, 152
  glazed tart, 197
  pears
    poached in cinnamon, 210
    poached in grape juice, 208
    sauteed with walnuts, 212
  and yogurt, 152
Fruit juices, distributors of, 35
Fudge sauce, 221

G

Glasses
  coded for alcoholic or non-
    alcoholic beverages, 64, 69,
    73
  separate shapes for wet and dry,
    54
Glögg, 186
Grand Marnier, substitutions for, 46
Grape juice, 34

H

Halloween Party, 103
Hard sauce, 200
  hot, 202
High tea
  American style, 59
  menu, 59
Holiday festivities, 96–107
Host/Hostess, hostile, 23
Hotels, meeting with caterer, 90

I

Ice cream, Bombe Desmond, 190
Icings
  butter: see hard sauce or filling for
    Parisian waffles
  cocoa, 230
  dark chocolate, 228
  French cream, 229
  fondant, 218

Indian pudding, 204
Invitations
  for cocktail party, 54
  dinner, 63
  lunch, 63
  for nonalcoholic event, 54

L

Lamb, marinade for, 164, 166
Lemon extract, substitutions for, 46
Lemon vinaigrette salad dressing,
  169
Light rum, substitutions for, 45
Liver
  devilled chicken, 140
  duck or chicken paté, 135
Lobster
  how to boil, 129
  how to tell if fresh, 128
  Newberg, 128
Lunch
  invitation to, 63
  menus, 111, 112
  in a restaurant, 79
  seating latecomers, 64
  the power (business jargon), 79

M

Madeira, substitutions for, 50
Mallon, James P., 13
Marinade
  for beef, 164
  for duck, 165
  for lamb, 164, 166
  for pork, 165
  for poultry, 165, 167
Marsala, substitutions for in
  zabaglione, 46
Mayonnaise, curry; see cold curry
  sauce
Meat, braising liquid for, 50
Meat loaf, 150
Menus
  breakfast, 108
  brunch, 109
  dinner, 113–114

lunch, 111, 112
supper; see also lunch and brunch
     menus, 115, 116
tea, 58–59
Cream tea Australian style, 59
High tea American Style, 59
High tea English style, 58
Meringue, soft, 195
Mixed parties, rules for, 70
Mulled apple juice, 181
Mushrooms
no-fat sautéed, 143
poached for sauce Newberg, 129
toasts, 153
Mussels
Aquarium supplies required for
     cleaning, 132
how to clean, 132
sauced without wine, 132

N

Never-drinkers, parties, 28
New Year's Eve party, 105
New Year's Day Buffet, 97
Nondrinkers
expectant mothers, 15
for health reasons, 15
recovering alcoholics, 15
for religious reasons, 15

O

Onions, for beef burgundy, 147
Orange extract, substitutions for, 46

P

Pancake Day, 98
Parisian Waffle Biscuits, 213
Parties, mixed drinkers and
     nondrinkers, rules for, 70
Party punch, 184
Party
Big Saturday Night
     space requirements for, 69
Christmas Day, 104
Christmas Eve, 104

cocktail, 52
invitation for, 55
new do's and don'ts, 52
diagram of room, 75
     arrangement, 74
Easter, 100
Halloween, 103
increased volume of food
     required for non-alcoholic,
     75
New Year's Eve, 105
New Year's Day leftovers, 97
nonalcoholic, invitation for
Pancake Day, 98
St. Patrick's Day, 91
Whitsunday, 101
sweet corner at, 72
tea, 56
Pasta, bacon noodle, cheese, and
     tomato casserole, 157
Paté
chicken liver, 155
coarse country; see meat loaf, 150
duck or chicken liver, 155
Pavlova, 194–196
Pears
poached in cinnamon, 210
poached in grape juice, 208
sautéed with walnuts, 212
Petits fours, 215
Pie, butterscotch, old fashioned,
     205
Plaice Fillets, poached with cream
     sauce, 134
Plum Pudding, 220
Poaching liquid for fish, 49
Popovers
savoury, 175
sweet, 175
variations, 176
Pork, marinade for, 165
Port, subtitutions for, 50
Potatoes, for Beef Burgundy, 147
Poultry
braising liquid for, 50
marinade for, 165
Puff Pastry cases, commercial
     frozen, 143

Punch
  bowls, 73
  how to label, 70
  Old English Norfolk, 35
  Party, 184

R

Raspberry juice, as substitute for
    Framboise, 44
Recipes, monitoring for Alcohol, 31
Restaurants
  dining in with recovering
      alcoholic, 88, 92
  non-alcoholic wines and beers
      in, 82
  techniques for successfully
      ordering alcohol-free food,
      92
Roquefort almond balls, 156
Rum, substitutes for, 45

S

Salad dressing
  blue cheese, 169
  vinaigrette, 169
Sandwiches
  fancy, 172
  fast, 177
Sauces
  alcohol in, 43, 67
  alcoholic ingredients and, 64
  cold curry, 163
  cream for shellfish, 168
  chocolate whipped cream, 192
  custard, 210
  fancy chocolate, 193
  foamy, 203
  fudge, 221
  hard sauce, 200
  hot hard sauce, 202
  tomato for pasta, 170, 224
  truffle, 171
  white, 121
  zabaglione cold for fruit, 224
Substitutions and alterations; see
    'flavour'
Scallops, Coquilles St. Jacques, 126

Seated events, 63
Seating, prearranged
  advantages of, 64
Shandy, 51
Sherry, substitutions for in
    savouries, 47
Shove Tuesday, see Pancake Day
Sirop de Fruits, 44
Slops, 57
Sorbet, sparkling apple, 199
Soup
  beef stock, quick, 124
  carrot, 118
  cauliflower, 119
  chicken stock, quick, 124
  cream of tomato, 121
  Lady Curzon, 123
Space requirements for large party,
    69
Spiced grape juice, 186
Spritzer
  blackberry juice, 42
  wine, 37
St. Patrick's Day party, 99
Stock
  beef, quick, 124
  chicken, quick, 124
Supper
  after theatre, 67
  late night, 115
  menus, 115, 116
  spring, 116
Syllabub, nonalcoholic, 182

T

Tea party, 56
Tea
  afternoon, 58
  American style, high, 59
  appropriate time of day, 56
  as a business engagement, 60
  Capers' spiced, 40
  cream, 58, 59
  as event favouring non-drinker,
      56
  high, 59
  iced, 39

power (business jargon), 60
sandwiches
    fancy, 172
    fast, 177
served in the office, 59
varieties of, 39
Toast, mushroom, 153
Tomato sauce for pasta, 170
Trifle, English, 206
    sherry substitute in, 46
    cream soda in, 46
Truffle sauce, 171

V

Vanilla
    the dilemma for recovering
        alcoholics, 187
    frozen cubes, 188
    substitutions for, 187–89
    sugar, 187
    syrup, 188
Vegetables
    for beef burgundy, 147

carrots, puréed, 179
Vinegar, wine, substitutions for, 48
Volleyballs, chicken vol-au-vents,
    143

W

Wet bar, 23, 53, 69, 73
Whipped cream, chocolate, 192
White sauce, for cream of tomato
    soup, 121
Whitsun Bank Holiday party, 101
Wine, nonalcoholic, 22, 36, 37
    alcohol content of, 22, 38
    correct placement, of, 30
Wine, red, substitutions for, 47
    spritzers, 37
    white, substitutions for, 46

Z

Zabaglione, 224
sauce, cold, for fruit, 224